Holding Back

Why we hide the truth about ourselves.

Special Note:

Quotations appearing in the following pages have been selected from Hazelden publications. For a complete listing of these titles consult the Reading List and order information at the end of this book.

About the author:

Marie Lindquist is the author of several wellness books for young adults. She lives in New York City.

Calligraphy by Theresa R. Nordby

Holding Back

Why we hide the truth about ourselves.

Marie Lindquist

Hazelden®

First published January, 1987.

Library of Congress Catalog Card Number:
86-082657

ISBN: 0-89486-419-X

Printed in the United States of America.

Editor's Note:
   Hazelden Educational Materials offers a variety
of information on chemical dependency and
related areas. Our publications do not necessarily
represent Hazelden or its programs, nor do they
officially speak for any Twelve Step organization.

CONTENTS

INTRODUCTION

INTRODUCTION

The search for the self begins with the first breath of life and endures through the last flicker of consciousness. A baby explores its world by trying to ingest it whole, stuffing toys, its own fingers, mother's pearls, and even the dog's ear into its mouth. What is inside the self is known and knowable. What is outside the self is mysterious, possibly unknowable, potentially dangerous.

Our first experiments at disclosing our inner selves are simple ones. We feel pain, hunger, or discomfort, and reveal those feelings by crying. Does the world respond quickly or not at all? Are our efforts rewarded? Ignored? Punished? Are our needs satisfied or thwarted?

These primitive experiments are part of the search for the self. The search goes on as we leave the crib, begin to walk, go to school, move through our rebellious teens, and mature into adults.

But when does the search for the self conclude? When do we step back and say, in effect, mission accomplished?

Whenever possible, I have alternated masculine and feminine pronouns in an effort to avoid repetitious "his or her" awkwardness.

Part I

Self and Society

For it is only by accepting

MYSELF

for what
I AM

that I may

DISCOVER

what I may

BECOME.

1
The Search for the Self

No discussion of self-disclosure can begin without a discussion of the self. What is this thing we carry within us, this complex collection of thoughts, memories, and traits we call the self?

Most of us have a strong sense of who we are, of what makes us individuals. Yet if someone gave you paper and pen and asked you to write *everything* about yourself, you'd find the task overwhelming. What lies inside each of us is as infinite as the universe. Exploring that inner realm is a task that lasts a lifetime.

When we are young, we yearn for the magic moment of being a grown-up. "I used to open my father's drawer," a male friend of mine once told me, "and just stood there breathing. That drawer, to me, held all the smells of a grown man — after-shave, tobacco, chalky tablets for ulcers. A few years ago, I opened my own drawer and found all the same smells. Does that mean I'm a grown-up at last? To the outside world, I guess I am. I have a house, a family. I pay my bills and handle my responsibilities. But inside, I don't feel finished at all."

The Chronological Self

So it is for most of us. The magic feeling of completeness never comes. And what a blessing that it doesn't, for the person who believes she is a finished product is in for real trouble.

5

The self is elastic, subject to change, open to revision and modification, right up until the last moment of life. This means that we can change to meet the unexpected crises of life; it means that parts of the self that cause pain, isolation, and sadness can be examined and, with determined effort, changed.

We are, at every moment, what we need to be if only we'd trust revealing our true selves, our centers, to one another.

Each Day a New Beginning
June 10

Self or Selves?

The self is never static. If you've ever asked someone a disturbing question or touched on a forbidden topic, you may have seen a rapid change take place: a narrowing of the eyes, a tensing of the mouth, a tightening of the facial muscles. Suddenly a great stone face appeared before you, letting you know, in no uncertain terms, that your question was quite inappropriate. Or you may have witnessed a different, but equally effective, transformation: a roll of the eyes, an "aw, shucks" scuffing of the toe, a disarming grin. In both cases, the person before you changed. The self you encountered one moment was not the same self revealed a moment later.

All of us are capable of these transformations. Like magicians, we change selves on an hour-to-hour, even minute-to-minute, basis. We are one person at work, another at home, a third alone. We are partners to our mates, parents to our children, children to our parents; we are advice-givers and advice-takers, trusted friends and formidable enemies. All in the course of one life, one week, one day.

The self you disclose to me is not necessarily the same self you disclose to your partner, your children, or your boss. Most of us grasp this idea with little difficulty. We know the self is multiple because experience tells us so.

But who are these others within us?

The answer to this question has puzzled philosophers for thousands of years. Mythology, religion, and literature mirror the multiple nature of man in larger-than-life dimensions: men are heroes or villians, angels or demons, saints or sinners; women are goddesses, whores, madonnas, amazons. In the past century, psychology has taken up the challenge.

Sigmund Freud divided the self into three parts: the id, the ego, and the superego. Yet anyone who has read Freud's work has discovered how difficult it is. The id, ego, and superego are as elusive as ghosts — it is hard to see how they relate to us and even harder to enlist them as allies in the search for self-awareness.

Another psychologist, the late Dr. Eric Berne,[1] founder of Transactional Analysis, came up with a model of the self that is simpler and far more useful than Freud's model. Like Freud, Berne also divided the self into three parts — three parts which he named the Parent, the Adult, and the Child. In Berne's scheme of things, these parts — which he called *ego states* — are present in all of us. Because I will be referring to Berne's useful, durable model throughout this book, a brief description of each ego state follows.

Your parents are telling you that someday you'll realize they were thinking of your future. They were concerned about the long-term effects on you.

When I Was Your Age
p.21

The Parent

The Parent is a storehouse of messages — messages we received from our own parents (or those who acted as parents) during our earliest years. Everything told to us was taken in and faithfully recorded by the Parent within us. *Pretty is as pretty does. Don't let your guard down. A job worth doing is worth doing well. Be a little man. Act like a lady.* All of the rules our parents passed along to us — wise or foolish, helpful or destructive — have been carefully saved.

The Parent ego state has saved not only our parents' words but their patterns of behavior. If we saw Father withdraw emotionally while Mother ran up huge bills, we recorded those "rules" too. *That's the way men are. That's the way women are. That's life!*

The Parent tells us how things are in the world and how we should *be* in that world. It's the set of rules, laws, and customs by which we plot our course through the tricky waters of life. Whenever we think or speak in absolutes such as *must, ought, should, always, never,* it is the Parent part of the self speaking, telling us how to act.

There are literally thousands of messages recorded in our Parent. A message such as *Don't spit on the floor,* contributes to our popularity throughout life, while messages such as *Don't be vulnerable* can get in our way.

We cannot alter the Parent because its messages were taught to us when we were too young to evaluate them. Nevertheless, we can overcome destructive Parent messages by listening to another important part of the self — the Adult.

Looking anew at the struggles that confound us and accepting responsibility for them doesn't lessen them, perhaps, but it does restore our personal power.

The Promise of a New Day
January 12

The Adult

If the Parent is the *taught* part of the personality, the Adult is the *thinking* part of it. The Adult

9

starts to emerge near the end of the first year of life, when the Child begins exploring his world and forming his own opinions about it.

"You can't go down those stairs," Mother says, and her words become one of the thousands of messages recorded in the Parent. But the crawling toddler soon learns the message is wrong. He can so go down the stairs!

If the Child falls down the stairs three out of four times he may examine the situation again and form yet another opinion: If I go down the stairs, I will probably hurt myself. Therefore, I *won't* go down the stairs.

So it goes as we master the stairs, learn new skills, choose a career, interact with others. The Adult is always there to question, monitor, and evaluate.

To have a well-developed Adult is to have a marvelous computer working on one's behalf. If the Parent says, *Opening up to people is dangerous,* the Adult is able to evaluate this teaching in the light of new data. Is opening up to people *always* dangerous? Can openness bring rewards as well as hazards? The Adult can override the negative, limiting message of the Parent. It can replace the old message with one that truly fits the situation. *Opening up to the wrong people can be dangerous, but opening up to the right people often brings rewards.*

The Parent is an archaic part of the personality, one formed during the first five years of life and immune to change thereafter. The Child, as we shall see later, is similarly archaic. *Only the Adult lives in the here and now.* Only the Adult gathers data in an ongoing way and puts

10

it to productive use. It is the actualized self, a self that can evaluate information and act on it.

> *Whether one has a sense of littleness because one is in fact little, or because one feels little, is all the same.*
>
> Self-Discovery in Recovery
> p. 24

The Child

Like the Parent, the Child within us is formed during the first few years of life. While the Parent recorded events taking place *outside* of us, the Child recorded all that was going on *inside.*

The Child is the feeling part of the self. It is the part that laughs genuine laughter and cries genuine tears. When we have an emotional response to an event, that response is coming from the Child within us.

Like the Parent, the Child does not analyze; it cannot put emotion-triggering events into perspective. The Child does not think, *Mother and Father love me very much, they are simply critical of the lipstick painting I have made on the wall.* No. She *feels* the weight of her parents' displeasure. *Father is angry! Mother does not love me! I am not okay!*

Because parents are faced with the tough task of civilizing their children, all of us receive many criticisms which make us feel "not okay" about ourselves. If our parents were good ones, we also received messages that made us feel okay. *You're a cute kid! How loving you are!*

11

It's good to be creative! If we were lucky enough to have parents like this, we can get about the business of life, strengthened by the fundamental belief that we are indeed okay.

But if we were raised by neglectful, abusive, or inadequate parents, the Child within us may remain fearful and isolated, frozen in the "not okay" position. The Child who was frequently criticized and made to feel bad about herself carries that burden into adult life. Small criticisms may send her into a tailspin. I am not okay! If others knew me as I really am, they would see that I am worthless! Unless the Adult intervenes to argue these points, the grown person is likely to go on feeling bad about herself, suffering as she did years ago when Mother and Father criticized her.

The Child is at once the most sensitive and most creative part of the self. The Parent may tell us that we should reach out to others and the Adult may confirm this by reasoning that the rewards of intimacy balance out the risks; but it is the Child whose yearning for closeness pushes us to action.

In a well-balanced, well-integrated person, the Parent, Adult, and Child ego states are of roughly equal size and power.

Rarely are these three ego states perfectly equal. A person who lacks the capacity for spontaneous self-disclosure is probably a person whose Parent outweighs her other ego states. A person who goes to the other extreme, sharing everything about herself without discrimination, is a person whose Child sits in the driver's seat.

12

Yet no matter how enlarged one of these ego states becomes, it can never squeeze out or obliterate the other states. The Parent, Adult, and Child are always within us, capable of surfacing at any moment. Each of these selves can communicate with the outside world. Not only that, these selves can communicate with each other. The Parent can make the Child feel not-okay. The Child can appeal to the Adult for protection. The Adult can override the dictatorial Parent.

I have introduced Berne's model here for two reasons. First, because it is easy to understand. In the few minutes you have been reading this even if you are coming upon this material for the first time, you have probably already identified chunks of the Parent, the Adult, and the Child within yourself, and that is marvelous indeed.

Berne's concept of the self is a useful one. It is a lens through which a wide variety of human problems can be brought into focus. Seeing the personality in this way can help almost any of us achieve deeper insights and thus improve the quality of our lives and our relationships.

Our
inner selves
have
messages
to give
and
messages
to receive
for the good
of all.

Each Day a New Beginning
June 9

2
Mixed Messages

Virtually all cultures, religions, and ethical systems place a high priority on openness. To share the self, to be open about one's thoughts and feelings, is perceived as good and right. Yet from the first moments of awareness, we receive mixed messages about revealing ourselves to others.

Civilization could not exist long unless we learned a little about the art of deception. The ability to keep at least *some* of our thoughts to ourselves is the grease that keeps the wheels of society turning. Business, national politics, and international negotiations rest equally on disclosure and concealment.

But isn't this hypocritical? Isn't deceptiveness the very poison that plagues modern life, keeping us from true intimacy? That's an easy conclusion to come to, but not a true one. If the ability to conceal ourselves was *all* negative, it would have dropped out of our repertoire long ago. No trait persists through the siftings of the generations unless it has some positive value.

Thousands of years ago, when primitive humans were struggling for dominance, the ability to conceal one's thoughts was a valuable asset. The person who could smile at an enemy was more likely to survive than the one who could not conceal animosity.

But does the ability to conceal our feelings serve us in our interactions with others as it served our primitive ancestors? Or has it merely become a burden — a no-longer-useful trait that causes pain, conflict, and alienation?

Although we now seldom find ourselves ringed by club-wielding enemies, we do find ourselves in stress-producing situations. Faced with such situations, the ability to conceal our feelings still comes into play as an effective coping mechanism.

If you have ever suffered a severe injury or found yourself in a life-threatening situation, you may have been astounded at what you *didn't* experience. For a moment you felt nothing at all. You moved and acted without awareness of pain or danger. Only when safety was reached did you begin to feel again.

Biologically, this lack of feeling serves a very real purpose. It allows one to act, unimpeded by pain, to meet the crisis. In a book called *Vital Lies, Simple Truths,*[1] psychologist Daniel Goleman suggests that the mind responds to psychological crises in a similar way. If a truth is too painful or too threatening to acknowledge, a kind of emotional numbing sets in. We suppress the truth because we are unable to cope with it. Goleman calls these deceptions "vital lies," necessary because they allow us to preserve the status quo of life.

While painful truths can be suppressed, they cannot be made to vanish completely. The mind is a leaky vessel indeed, and buried truths are likely to manifest themselves in a host of physical and psychological ills. All of us have, at some time, shied away from a truth too painful to acknowledge. We have held that truth within us, buried under layers of denial, until the repercussions of withholding became as difficult and painful as the truth itself.

Lying can be like sailing choppy waters. The more we lie, the higher the waves get, and the harder the sailing.

Today's Gift
December 30

The Abuse of Openness

The Idea that it might be anything less than deeply neurotic to withhold parts of the self strikes most people as something akin to heresy. We live in a society that has made a fetish of self-revelation; we have been indoctrinated to see all, tell all, and reveal all about ourselves — or, at least, to *believe* that seeing all, telling all, and revealing all is what we should constantly be about.

As a result of this, we are deluged with confessions: celebrities drag their personal crises before us in the media, casual acquaintances force their problems upon us.

But is this kind of "openness" truly helpful?

The truth is, this isn't openness at all, but a sort of obsessive confessionalism that leads nowhere. Random disclosures have little meaning and do little to enhance our lives. If a virtual stranger reveals herself to me the act begins and ends there. There is no context surrounding the disclosure, nothing which makes it memorable or meaningful. There is no foundation of intimacy between us, no "before" and "after." Since we will soon go our separate ways, there is no future in which to harvest the rewards and shoulder the responsibilities of the disclosure. The release is all short-term, a quick fix with no lasting effect.

In this atmosphere, self-disclosure often becomes a way of clinging to problems rather than solving them. The woman who constantly announces her anger about men has adopted anger-about-men as a fixed life position. Anger becomes her guiding force, the pole star her life revolves around. *Here is what you should know about me,* her confessions tell us; *I am angry because this, this, and this happened to me. Expect me to act, think, and react in an angry, embittered way.* For this person, the role of Angry Woman becomes self-perpetuating, and her repetitious confessions strengthen rather than weaken her performance.

Similarly, the man who announces his difficulties with intimacy to the new woman in his life may only seem to be making a gesture towards closeness. In reality, he may be hedging his bets for the future. Then, if the relationship fails to achieve the hoped for level of intimacy, he can absolve himself of responsibility. *Don't blame me — I told you I wasn't any good at this!*

If this is a book about the rewards of self-disclosure, why should we bother to even glance at the other side of the coin? Because it is important to realize that the ability to conceal one's feelings has a valid place in the human drama, just as the ability to share one's feelings has. Failing to disclose one's true self can — and often does — serve a legitimate purpose.

Moreover, all self-disclosure is not uniformly good. The purpose of self-disclosure is to deepen the foundations of intimacy by sharing *something* significant with *someone* significant. The purpose of self-disclosure is to, as Fritz Perls[2] wrote, "own one's own feelings" — to lay claim to one's secrets in a way that promotes awareness and well-being.

It is necessary for each of us to explore how we make disclosures and understand what our underlying motives are. We are obligated not simply to blurt out the truth about ourselves but to select the paths of disclosure that release us from old patterns and allow us to go on with the business of living full, productive, and loving lives.

Part II:

The Separated Self

...the more we allow
OTHERS
to really know US,
the greater will be
our opportunities
for GROWTH
and HAPPINESS.

Our secrets
burden us.

3
Dark Deceptions

All of us deceive ourselves and others on a regular basis. We withhold thoughts and feelings, we cover up the truth about our inner conflicts and desires. Sometimes these deceptions are harmless and even helpful, justified by the situation of the moment.

But deceptions that become a permanent part of our lives are crippling. If we withhold our true selves from everyone, then we can achieve true intimacy with no one. Not only that, we cannot even achieve intimacy with ourselves, for only through open and honest communication with others can we truly know ourselves.

Deceptions like this are far from harmless. They are the big lies we tell about ourselves, ones that go beyond the tactful fibs of the social and business worlds. Not telling one's boss about an extra glass of wine at lunch may be simply prudent, but denying a large-scale drinking problem is a crippling denial. Such deceptions do not honor the need for privacy, nor do they contribute to psychological health. In fact, they do just the opposite.

I call these lies dark deceptions because of the deep and impenetrable shadow they cast over our lives. Whenever we *consistently* withhold a major truth about ourselves, sharing it with no one, we are engaging in a dark deception.

Dark deceptions can be told about a variety of truths, to a variety of people, for a variety of reasons. The reasons, however, always have one thing in common: they are essentially selfish and self-serving. Although we often convince ourselves that we are withholding the truth for legitimate reasons — such as getting along with others or protecting others' feelings — this is not really the case. Dark deceptions revolve around <u>self-oriented motives</u> such as the ones listed here.

- We need to feel all-powerful.
- We need to feel perfect.
- We need to feel superior to those around us.
- We need to control the feelings of others.
- We need the approval of everyone.
- We need to feel that others cannot challenge us.
- We need to deny the legitimacy of our problems.

There are other reasons why we withhold the truth about ourselves, but you probably get the idea already. As you can see, the key word in each of these statements is *need*. We engage in dark deceptions because we feel needy and inadequate; because, for one reason or another, we do not feel able to cope with life as it really is. We do not feel lovable enough to find acceptance in spite of our faults; we do not feel strong enough to confront and resolve our problems.

Consequences of Withholding

Everyone knows that actions have consequences. A rock pushed from the top of a hill rolls to the bottom, scattering pebbles and flattening grass as it goes. An angry word leaves a mark in the heart of another.

It is less easy to see that actions *not* taken also have consequences. Yet they do. Results flow from the things we don't do just as they flow from the things we do. When we withhold important parts of ourselves, we trigger a chain reaction.

Secrets diminish self-respect; they foster paranoia, and they make it impossible to have honest and open communication.

The Promise of a New Day
August 30

If you have ever carried a fearful secret within you, you have probably experienced anxiety, sadness, and even rage as a consequence. But did you stop to ask yourself where these powerful feelings came from? Probably not. Most of us don't. We simply go on shouldering the burden, blaming our suffering on the secret within us.

Yet that secret, whatever it is, is seldom the true source of our pain. The grief we feel is not the result of our secret but of our failure to be honest and open. Withholding brings its own

25

set of consequences that branch out to affect every part of our lives.

Twelve common consequences of withholding include:

1. *Loss of community with others.* When you withhold parts of yourself, you cut away the common ground that binds you to others. By denying your own problems you are, in part, denying your own humanity. It is human not only to be imperfect but to acknowledge those imperfections. People who avoid self-disclosure do so by barricading themselves, armoring their souls against the world. Safe inside this fortress, they become isolated and cut off, an island cut off from the continent of humanity.

2. *Formation of superficial relationships.* Relationships grow little by little, deepening by stages as the two people involved reveal themselves to each other. Sharing something about yourself often triggers the same response in the other person. Intimacy, based on trust and acceptance, grows out of this kind of progressive sharing. But the process is thwarted if one person cannot or will not share the inner self with the other. Withholding invites withholding. When the true self is withheld from another, their relationship ceases to grow. It remains superficial because one person has, in effect, said to the other, "I am not willing to reveal more of myself to you. I do not trust you." This may be completely appropriate for some kinds of relationships, such as business alliances or casual friendships. But if you approach every relation-

ship in this way, it is very likely you will never know the delights of true intimacy.

> *We cheat ourselves of the real pleasure in living when we hold ourselves back from someone close.*
>
> The Promise of a New Day
> June 12

3. *Devaluation of intimacy.* The person who loves another yet withholds significant parts of himself creates a kind of counterfeit intimacy. The love the withholder receives from others is devalued because it is not based on reality. People who withhold themselves from their loved ones often think, "If they knew me as I really am, they wouldn't love me at all." The withholding person fears losing the love and regard of others. But by failing to disclose himself, he deprives himself of the very thing he seeks to preserve.

4. *Robs others of love and understanding.* The withholding person has a skewed sense of priorities. Defending her secret becomes a primary concern, and difficult choices often force her to choose *for* her secret and *against* others in her life. A mother who abuses her child and denies her problem also denies her child love and understanding. When we ask ourselves who withholding harms, we must look beyond ourselves to the others in our lives.

5. *Kills spontaneity and joy.* The person who harbors a secret lives in a limbo of waiting. He is always on the alert, fearful that someone will probe too close. He is on guard for the moment when he must flee or be discovered. Inside each of us is a natural Child, the part of the personality that knows spontaneity and joy. When we adopt a withholding position, we stifle the Child within us, for the open and honest Child cannot be trusted to keep secrets. Instead, we give control to the harsh, judgmental Parent part of the personality. The Parent rules with an iron hand — it must, if precious secrecy is to be maintained. When this happens, we become rigid in defense of our secret; unable to act spontaneously, unable to interact freely with others, and unable to know true joy.

6. *Arrests personal growth.* Why do we keep something about ourselves a secret? Not because it poses a problem for others, but because it poses a problem for *us*. What we have difficulty acknowledging is usually the very thing we need to confront and resolve. When a problem is resolved, it vanishes from our lives. Problems that are not acknowledged cannot be resolved. Our denial gives them a permanent place in our lives. Whatever strides we make in other areas, our troubled secrets remain, awesome and powerful, roadblocks that we can never quite get around.

7. *Limits life options.* When we deny parts of ourselves and refuse to confront them, we are limiting the options we have in life. There are things we cannot do, must not do, or never

28

have the opportunity to do because of the unre-solved conflicts we hide deep inside us. The person who eats compulsively lives a life limited by preoccupation with food and a weight problem. The alcoholic who does not confront the problem may lose out on job opportunities, or on the love of friends and family. The part of ourselves we deny is often the reason our choices in life are limited.

8. *Wastes time and energy.* A person who withholds from others creates a false self-image. It takes both time and energy to maintain this false image. Our time on earth, just as the resource of personal energy, is limited. We misuse our resources when we devote them to bolstering the false image we have created. Time we might have spent working, loving, or enjoying ourselves is wasted; energy we might have used to learn a new skill or absorb a new idea is siphoned away.

9. *Thwarts purposes and goals.* Healthy, happy people have a sense of purpose. They believe life is worthwhile, that they have something positive to contribute to the world. These are the achievers of life, whether their goals mandate writing a symphony or simply loving their partners, children, and friends in the fullest possible way. The person who denies significant parts of herself lacks the freedom needed to pursue and realize her goals. She may achieve much in her lifetime, but she will never realize her full potential as a human being.

10. *Loss of sense of self.* The person who withholds part of himself does, in effect, deny

part of his own personality. He becomes divided against himself. This self-alienation leads to a loss of self-esteem, for how can we feel good about ourselves when parts of us are too ugly to even acknowledge? To the outside world, we may be winners in every sense of the word. But the withholding person is always a loser to himself, laboring under the burden of self-denial and secrecy.

11. *Contributes to physical ills.* Mind and body are not separate components but integrated parts of the self. The wear and tear of denying part of the personality, of guarding one's inner self from others, takes a toll on the body. Anxiety-induced aches and upsets, panic attacks, obsessive or compulsive behaviors or both — are all likely to trouble the withholding person.

12. *Ensures that pain will continue.* We withhold and deny the truth about ourselves because we fear the pain of disclosure. Yet as long as we remain in this false position, isolated from ourselves and from others, we experience pain that is just as real. The act of withholding ensures only one thing — our pain and loneliness will continue. Thus we inflict on ourselves the very thing we are trying to avoid. With time, we may grow so comfortable with our burden that we cannot imagine life without it.

Each of these consequences represents a loss of one kind or another — loss of intimacy, loss of self-awareness, and loss of one's potential as a human being. When we withhold significant parts of ourselves from others, we feel grief or anger or both. These feelings are not neurotic — in fact, they are just the opposite. Our grief is healthy, a sign that we are human enough and feeling enough to long for what we have traded away in our quest for secrecy.

Hiding nothing
convinces us
that we have
nothing to hide,

thus we're free
to try
new behaviors,
move in
unfamiliar
directions.

The Promise of a New Day
September 18

4

What Are You Hiding?

The withholding person has at her core something she seeks to hide from others. Sometimes, the person knows exactly what her fearful secret is.

I once had a friend who, as a child, had been sexually abused by an uncle. Like all victims of this kind of abuse, she grew up feeling both bad and guilty about herself. She believed that what had gone on was her fault, proof of her essential worthlessness as a human being. I knew Maureen for several years without knowing this part of her.

Then, one day, we heard that a friend's child had been approached and fondled by a stranger. Maureen's calm exterior dissolved before my eyes. Her whole story came pouring out in a torrent, as vividly recalled as if it had happened only yesterday. Each detail was frozen in her mind — right down to the smell of her uncle's cologne and the television program in the next room. Five minutes later, Maureen sank back in her chair, drained and exhausted. I reached out and put my hand over hers. "My God," Maureen said, glancing around the room in disbelief. "I thought the world would fall apart if I ever told anyone that!"

For over thirty years Maureen carried her secret inside her. All this time she remembered the scent of cologne and the blare of the television set. For over thirty years, she remembered

and relived every moment of that long-ago
afternoon.

---

*The people in our lives have ears
to listen and arms to hold us -- if
we choose to open the windows
to our souls.*

Night Light
June 10

Maureen and I had often talked about relationships, and she often said she had difficulty
trusting men. As reasons for this, she had of-
fered everything from a broken engagement
during her college years to the divorce between
her parents. Yet none of these insights, for all
the marvelous sense they made, had brought
her one step closer to overcoming her problem.

As I sat across from my friend, the real reason
for her difficulties became obvious. "The funny
thing was," Maureen concluded, "I didn't feel
sorry for myself at all. Mostly, I felt bad for my
aunt, because she was married to him."

Maureen might not have felt sorry for herself
at the time, but when she grew up she dis-
trusted every man she became involved with. It
was her way of protecting herself, of making
sure she would never find herself in her aunt's
position.

34

> *Evading an issue, by refusing to make a decision, never solves anything. It only keeps us in a state of helplessness, despair, and fear.*
>
> The Reflecting Pond
> p. 20

Some people, like Maureen, are in full possession of their secrets. Others aren't so aware. They may have only a vague sense of the truths they withhold. They have pushed the *real* issue so far from them that it has become blurred and indistinct. Or they have diverted themselves by inventing other problems — false ones — to focus upon.

I heard an example of this one night as I listened to a radio talk show. A woman called to complain about her nonexistent love life. "I go out," she said, "I'm active, I meet dozens of men, but none of them are interested in me because I'm short." The host, a highly intuitive man, cut her off in mid-protest. Short? *Short?* It seemed highly unlikely that shortness was the lady's real problem.

After a moment's pause, the host gently asked the woman how much she weighed. Defensiveness bristled through the phone wires. "That's not the problem," the woman snapped angrily. In this way, she unwittingly revealed what her problem was — extra pounds that left her feeling defensive and unlovable.

35

Even over the phone, the woman's problem was evident, just as it must have been to anyone meeting her. Yet she was only vaguely aware of the truth about herself. Like Garfield the cat, she had convinced herself that she wasn't overweight, just under-tall! She had pushed the real issue away so often, had spun such a complex web of denial and rationalization, that she had lost sight of the real issue. In her mind, the source of her problems was her shortness — which, of course, she was powerless to do anything about.

Still other people have no sense of withholding anything at all, for their truths are buried deep in the subconscious. These people are the master secret-keepers, able to deceive not only those around them but, to a certain extent, themselves as well.

What's the harm in this? Isn't it true, "What you don't know won't hurt you?" Not at all. While these people may have buried their secrets in the subconscious, the subconscious is still part of the self. People who aren't aware of their own withholding natures still suffer the repercussions of holding back.

In many ways, the dilemma these master secret-keepers face is more frustrating and puzzling than the dilemma faced by those who are aware of their secrets. Before these people can resolve their feelings of discomfort and pain, they must first unearth the secrets within themselves.

> *Trapped feelings are like birds in a cage, or a rabbit in a trap, they try to get out any way they can.*

Today's Gift
March 23

Symptoms of Withholding

In Chapter Three, I discussed some of the *consequences* of withholding, ways in which the failure to disclose ourselves to others gets in the way of happiness and fulfillment. Here are some *symptoms* of withholding — behavior patterns that can tip you off to unresolved, even unacknowledged, conflicts within yourself.

- *Emotional peaks and valleys.* Powerful surges of emotion that are not grounded in reality; sudden letdowns that do not seem to have any cause.
- *Numbness.* Exactly the opposite of the situation described above. In this case, one feels emotionally dead; real events that should trigger joy or sorrow arouse no response at all.
- *Oversensitivity.* An emotional response that is much stronger than the situation warrants.
- *Diminished emotions.* Again, the opposite of the situation above. In this case, emotional responses are only half felt, as if the person were afraid of giving full vent to his feelings.

- *Intrusive thoughts.* Thoughts that seem to "come from nowhere," unbidden and unwanted.
- *Inappropriate responses.* A reaction or feeling that is wrong for the situation, such as the person who feels guilty or even sad when given a compliment. A person who responds inappropriately is not reacting to external events but is responding to her own internal stimuli.
- *Obsession.* Deliberately dwelling on a thought, memory, or image. Preoccupation with something that has nothing to do with immediate surroundings.
- *Compulsion.* The irresistible urge to repeat some behavior pattern. In this case, one seems to act against his own will.
- *Overalertness.* Extreme nervousness, as if the body is constantly on red alert, waiting for an expected attack.
- *Sleep disturbances.* Insomnia, sudden waking in the middle of the night, bad dreams, waking up feeling exhausted — all can be signs of an uneasy mind. When the consciousness relaxes its hold, the troubled subconsciousness seeks to unburden itself.
- *Missed associations.* The person who avoids drawing conclusions seems to have a mental "blind spot." She does not see the "cause and effect" nature of things and has no sense that her own actions shape her life.
- *Skewed view of reality.* A faulty interpretation of what is going on; misunderstand-

ing the attitudes and intentions of others. A good example of this is the person who feels others are judging him, deciding against him, when just the opposite is true.

- *Inability to concentrate.* Inability to focus one's attention on the immediate situation or the task at hand. Thoughts keep drifting off "in all directions," as if the mind is trying to distract itself.

- *Disavowal.* Denial that things are the way they are, refusal to accept a fact even in light of overwhelming evidence that it is so.

- *Memory Lapses.* Broken chain of recollection; difficulty in recalling the past or the inability to recall it accurately.

- *Magical thinking.* Not being able to see the difference between wish and reality. Believing that what one hopes to be true *will* be true.

- *Perpetual daydreaming.* Using fantasy to block out thoughts and feelings.

- *Free-floating anxiety.* General discomfort and distress. He feels that something is wrong but is unable to identify the source of the trouble.

- *Misplaced anger.* Rage that is not caused by real events or situations. Often, the anger is directed at a convenient scapegoat — the boss or partner, fate, the system, members of the opposite sex, and so on.

- *Depression.* Depression is anger turned inward. In this case, the kind of causeless

anger described above is unleashed on
the self.

- *Detachment.* Feeling that he is observing
  his own life rather than living it.
- *Shifting ego states.* The Parent, Adult, and
  Child aspects of the personality appear at
  inappropriate times. The person bent on
  avoiding responsibility gives vent to her
  playful — but irresponsible — Child; the
  partner, fearful of intimacy, lets her Parent
  take control.
- *Extreme passivity.* He does not take action
  or move ahead with life.
- *Extreme restlessness.* She fills her time
  with meaningless activity, as if trying to
  keep herself, literally, too busy to think.

Some of these symptoms — such as disor-
dered sleep, free-floating anxiety, and misdirected anger — are stress reactions. They are
direct responses to what is going on in the inner
world of the self.

Other symptoms — like missed associations,
perpetual daydreaming, or compulsive behavior — are escape mechanisms. They are things
we do to *block* (escape from) stress reactions.

The problem with escape mechanisms is that
they work. They *do* soothe and distract us, and
because they are so effective, we soon come to
rely on them.

And this is where the trouble begins. While
escape mechanisms allow us to run away from
stress reactions, they do nothing to help us get
rid of them. When we lose ourselves in busy-
work or engage in magical thinking (two more

escape mechanisms) we are doing nothing to change the situation.

Relying on escape mechanisms only compounds our troubles, for while these mechanisms interfere with stress, they also interfere with the business of life itself.

None of these "symptoms" is conclusive in itself. Each may make only a passing (and therefore insignificant) appearance in our lives. But when one of these traits becomes permanent, it is a sign something is wrong.

The problem may not be an undisclosed secret — many of these symptoms come about as a result of other problems, too. Yet stress reactions and their antidotes — escape mechanisms — are worth looking into. For whatever reason, they are limiting our potential and keeping us from full enjoyment of our lives.

Our PROGRESS
and our SUCCESS
in life is both
measured and
nurtured by the
number of genuine
contacts we make
with the men
and women
who are sharing
our space in time.

5

The Withholding Personality

Who am I?
Who are they?
Who do they see when they look at me?
Who do I want them to see?
Who makes the rules?

These are questions we begin asking ourselves during the first years of life. Even before we take our first steps or mouth our first words, we are busy solving the puzzle of who we are.

We yearn to know what others think of us. Are we smart? Pretty? Handsome? Likable? Good? Destined to go far in life? Or are we selfish, lazy, ugly, and dumb? The answers we arrive at, based on countless interactions with the all-important big people in our lives, will shape the self-image we carry into adulthood.

The Divided Self

"We come to earth," as William Wordsworth said, "trailing clouds of glory."[1] As infants, our responsibilities are few. We sleep, wake, cry, and eat. Usually, these simple actions are enough to win the love and approval of those around us.

But it is not long until the magic wears off. Before much time has passed, we learn that love and approval are conditional. As immature members of society, there are many things we must do to be loved — and just as many things that we *must not* do. We learn that many of our natural impulses are unacceptable; sure to win disapproval.

Because we crave love and because our survival depends on pleasing the adults around us, we become adept at repressing these unacceptable impulses. Without consciously thinking about it, we learn to hide whole portions of our natures.

From the very beginning, society teaches us that we have two selves: A *good* self that can be brought out into the light and shown to others, and a *bad* self that must be kept locked up.

The divided self exists in all of us. Even people who have mastered the monumental task of loving themselves have a sense of their own dark sides. People learn they can best conquer their dark sides not by denying or repressing them, but by acknowledging and facing them.

What separates the self-lovers from the self-haters among us? Are their bright sides brighter? Are their dark sides darker? Not necessarily. People who love themselves have an innate sense of their own humanness. They do not see their dark sides as grotesquely inhuman, separating them from the rest of humanity. Just the opposite — they accept this very human part of themselves.

When we make the time and effort to know ourselves, it encourages others to want to know us, too.

Today's Gift
December 2

44

People who have low self-esteem, who hate themselves and hide themselves away from others, have never made this leap of faith. They do not accept their own dark nature; they keep it at arm's length, convinced it separates them from the rest of the world.

In a very real sense, these people are more severely divided against themselves than others. For them, the barrier between good and bad selves is impenetrable, a partition mined with explosives and barbed wire.

How We Learn: The Life Script

Open. Honest. Self-disclosing. Intimate. Loving. We are born to be all these things. They are natural human impulses.

Withholding. Self-deceptive. Secretive. Isolating. Denying. We are born to be none of these things. They are not natural impulses, but behaviors we learn as we go through life. Often, we learn them so well they become our only way of functioning.

How do we learn to withhold and deny the self?

We learn over a period of years, as a response to all that is going on around us.

Much of what we learn comes from our parents — or from the people in our lives who function as parents. That doesn't mean our parents are conscious of all they convey to us. No mother decides to "teach" her daughter self-hatred, just as no father decides to undermine his son's sense of self-esteem.

But that is often what happens. As children, we are extremely sensitive to the world around

45

us. We make decisions based on the outcome of daily events. Yet because our powers of insight and evaluation are limited, we often draw the wrong conclusion. We "learn" the wrong lesson.

A family is like a windchime; each member hangs in delicate balance with the others.

Today's Gift
September 2

In Bobby's family, Mother and Father were frequently at war with each other. Their fights were extremely upsetting to Bobby, who found love and friendship in Aunt Joan, Mother's older sister. After a particularly disruptive fight, Bobby went to Aunt Joan for comfort.

When news of this got back to Bobby's mother, she was furious. *What a bad boy! How could you be so stupid? Never tell people about fights your father and I have!*

Mother, beset with her own problems, felt she was asking for something quite reasonable: privacy. But Bobby was too young to understand that. Instead, he saw the incident *only* from his own point of view. *I am bad! I am stupid! I am bad and stupid for sharing my feelings with Aunt Joan!*

His mother's harsh words "taught" Bobby the wrong lesson. Instead of deciding to *respect Mother's privacy,* Bobby decided something quite different. He decided to *bottle up troubled feelings.*

46

Usually, no one event shapes the course of an entire life, but the interplay of many such events does. If Bobby's mother was simply having a bad day, the incident will probably become unimportant. But if Bobby is continually shamed and punished for not hiding his feelings, his decision to *bottle up troubled feelings* will be immeasurably reinforced. It will become one of the many, many messages he carries into adult life.

All of these messages, gathered from the all-powerful adults around us, give us a rudimentary blueprint for life. Eric Berne[2] called this blueprint a *life script*. Each of us has such a script, and the script is all-encompassing. It governs how we spend our time, which of our ego states is strongest, how we go about work and play, whom we love and how we love them, whether we are self-disclosing or self-withholding, even how long we expect to live and what we expect people to say about us after we die.

The life script is written by the child in response to the outside world — an arrangement that leaves all sorts of room for error. By the time we start school, we have already decided whether openness is good or bad; indeed, we have already decided whether we will be open with others or not.

Most of us are, at this very minute, living by decisions we made thirty, fifty, even seventy years ago. What if we made the wrong decision? The life script can be changed, but only through a conscious effort of the will. And before that can be done, we must bring the script from the unconsciousness, where it is born, into the realm of consciousness.

The Life Script in Action

Unless we have spent a lot of time in therapy or enlightened self-examination, most of us aren't aware of our personal life scripts. For most people, the script will remain locked in the unconsciousness, an invisible set of rules by which major decisions are made.

How can we discover our personal script? It isn't easy. In fact, we need to turn detective to track it down.

Although life varies from year to year and decade to decade, we change very little. We tend to act in certain predictable ways, choosing the same course of action and achieving the same results over and over again.

These patterns of behavior are important clues in tracking down the life script. Once we are aware of them, we're well on the way to solving the puzzle.

Unfortunately, most of us are so blind to our own actions that we can't see the forest for the trees. Our patterns of behavior may be crystal clear to others. To us, they remain a mystery. For example, all of us know some man or woman with a talent for falling in love with the wrong person. To our friend, this is just a matter of bad luck. But to us, it's anything *but* bad luck — it takes a great deal of know-how to pick the wrong person time after time!

Broadening our vision so that we may see life from a stranger's perspective heightens the clarity of our own, and sharing the view bonds us, deepens all meaning, and closes the gap that lies between.

The Promise of a New Day
November 28

Friends can be invaluable in helping us become aware of our own life scripts. So can loving strangers — the kind of people you find in self-help and support groups. By helping us see what we do over and over again, they can help us identify the script we live by.

A woman named Marlys lived more than half her life without understanding how her personal script shaped it. At the age of 40, she joined a group and began to explore her problems. Marlys, an alcoholic, also complained about being "numb" — out of touch with her own feelings.

After a trip home to see her parents, Marlys told the group this story.

"While I was home, my mother did something that upset me — hurt my feelings — very much. I guess I overreacted because it reminded me of the way I had been treated as a child. Instead of saying nothing, as I always had, I told my mother she had hurt me.

49

"Well, the sky just about opened up! My mother was beside herself — how could I make her feel so bad, so inadequate? Wouldn't I please, *please* say something to make her feel better? Couldn't I see how bad she felt? She made a terrible scene — just like she did when I was little!"

As someone in the group pointed out, it isn't hard to see what had happened to Marlys. During her childhood, Marlys faced this situation over and over again. Whenever she showed her hurt feelings to her mother, she was punished not once but twice. First, her own feelings were discounted — treated as if they simply didn't matter. Second, Marlys was forced to take responsibility for her mother's injured feelings.

While she was feeling hurt, Marlys was put in the position of making the person who had hurt her feel better. Is it any wonder that she learned to ignore her own feelings, to silence them by washing them away with alcohol?

At a young age, Marlys decided feelings were dangerous. This decision became an important part of her life script — a "Don't Get Close" script that kept Marlys isolated from herself and from others well into middle age.

Given the situation during Marlys's childhood, her script made sense. Feelings *were* dangerous, just as getting close to her mother was. But thirty years later, this decision made no sense at all. Marlys *wanted* to get close to others, to feel her own feelings. Yet she couldn't because she was still living by her old life script.

In Marlys's case, the group helped her identify her life script. By sharing this part of herself with others she became free to break the spell she was under. She was able to make new decisions and create a new script for herself, one that was productive and rewarding rather than self-destructive.

The Withholding Escalator

There are some things only we can do for our emotional, physical, and spiritual health: eat right, exercise, get plenty of rest, pray and meditate on a daily basis. Yet there are needs we cannot take care of alone: solving all our problems, comforting ourselves, developing intimacy with others, feeling loved and cared for. Those things need to come from others.

Night Light
March 19

When we have a life script that tells us we are bad, that we dare not disclose ourselves to others, that feelings are dangerous, we are under a spell — a spell that will damage our lives unless we can break loose as Marlys did.

If we cannot break loose, we step on an escalator that is always going up. The more we withhold about ourselves, the more we feel we *must* withhold.

The person who has a withholding life script often failed to receive the support, nurturance, and acceptance needed during childhood. His parents, whom he looked on as infallible, reinforced the idea that he was unacceptable, unworthy, and unlovable.

In an attempt to win their approval, the child decided to suppress the unacceptable parts of himself — to disclose his true self to no one. Needless to say, the attempt was usually a futile one, for parents capable of creating such feelings of unworthiness in their children are usually *incapable* of freely showing their love. The tragedy is — in most cases — these parents *do* love their children. They are not purposely cruel. Rather, they are hampered by their own insecurities and limitations.

Unfortunately, children are unaware of their parents' human failings. To the child, Mother and Father are both judge and jury. If these all-knowing people find him unlovable, then he must be unlovable indeed.

As life goes on, this person casts the whole world in the role of his negative, unloving parents. He is careful never to reveal too much of himself to anyone lest he be shamed and rejected. He may seek distraction and fulfillment from a variety of sources, both good and bad: work, shopping, drugs, alcohol, food, gambling, exercise, hobbies, volunteerism, and intellectual pursuits. But even the best of these

52

alternatives are devoid of the kiss of human intimacy. They cannot bring the person the validation he needs.

For the person with a withholding life script, isolation becomes both a defense and a punishment. The more he hides himself from others, the more he is deprived of acceptance and love. The more deprived he is, the more unworthy he feels. The more unworthy he feels, the more withholding he becomes. The escalator goes up and up, stopping only when the person gains the courage to acknowledge — and embrace — his long-disowned self.

HAPPINESS

is something we all deserve. However, there are often preparatory steps we need to take, a number of which will not bring joy, before we arrive at a place of sustained happiness.

6

Payoffs and Secondary Gains

Miller, a man in his fifties, has tried to stop drinking several times. Although he has never succeeded, Ann, his wife, has stayed in the marriage.

"I want to get sober," Miller confides. "God knows, I'm trying. It just doesn't seem to work. Annie's a saint."

"I'm not a saint," his wife insists. "I think about leaving all the time. You can't imagine what it's been like all these years. This time, my mind is made up — either *he* gets sober or *I* get out."

What happens next? Not much. Miller tries to stop drinking one more time — and fails one more time. As for Annie, the saint, she's right there with him. "I can't leave him when he's trying so hard," she reasons, postponing her plans and laying aside her threats.

Both Miller and his wife are desperately unhappy, as they'll tell anyone who has time to listen. They're unhappy with life, and unhappy with each other. Most of all, they're unhappy with their own inability to change.

Why do people persist in behavior patterns that keep them unhappy and unfulfilled?

Let's look at Miller and Ann a little more closely. They've been married for more than thirty years — no small accomplishment. From the standpoint of sheer longevity, their marriage is successful. On a day-to-day, year-to-year basis, it works.

How it works is another matter. After so many years, a pattern has evolved. When Miller's drinking begins to get out of hand, Ann tries to hold things together. She makes excuses to his boss, hides the truth from their friends, and turns a deaf ear to the verbal abuse he heaps on her.

Things quickly reach an unmanageable state. That's when Ann enters a stage of her own: begging and pleading. She will do anything for Miller if only he will stop drinking. Anything at all. And if he can't — well, this time she really *will* leave him. Her cries fall on deaf ears, of course. Miller's drinking gets worse and worse.

Then comes The Crisis. Sometimes it is the loss of a job, sometimes an arrest on a drunken driving charge. Now Miller is really down. He's hit bottom. Sorrowfully, he begs Ann to help him out one more time, promising this time things will be different.

Ann flies into action. She calls hospitals, treatment clinics, psychiatrists. She finds out what their insurance will cover and what it won't. She calls Alcoholics Anonymous and is relieved to find there's still a daily meeting nearby — just as there was during Miller's last crisis.

After drying out, Miller is charged with new confidence. This time it really worked. This time, he's *really* changed. That's why he checks out of the hospital early, stops seeing his therapist, and junks the literature his wife got from

A.A. Because he's cured, he doesn't need any of those things.

Miller is now in control of himself. So there's no harm in having one little drink with the guys, is there? Or a few to ring in the New Year? Or a few more to celebrate whatever occasion is at hand?

Ann, of course, sees the danger in this. "How can you even think of drinking, after all I've done for you?" she accuses. It doesn't help. Soon the whole pattern is in motion again.

"I want to stop drinking," Miller complains, "but it never seems to work out."

"I'm going to leave," Ann says grimly. "I can't take much more of this."

The truth is, Ann can — and will — take a lot more. As for Miller, he'll go right on drinking because drinking is what he *wants* to do.

For both partners, this nightmarish situation has a number of rewards.

Let's look at Miller's side of it first. He enjoys drinking. He likes the lift it gives his spirits and the way it anesthetizes his anxiety and insecurity. He likes the aura of drama and excitement it gives his life. The truth is: Miller has always found sobriety dull and empty.

By periodically "trying" to get sober, Miller has found a way to enjoy the best of both worlds. He can drink without feeling guilty about it and, at the same time, feel proud of himself for the valiant battle he's putting up. What a guy! Isn't it too bad? It's just his cross to bear.

This pattern of trying and failing also wins a lot of sympathy and support from his wife. "Just try, dear, that's all I ask," is Ann's attitude. After thirty-plus years, Miller knows good and well she's not *really* going to leave him.

There are plenty of other benefits, too. As long as Miller is struggling with alcohol, he doesn't have to take responsibility for much else in life. Forget about advancing in his career — for Miller, just *keeping* a job is what it's all about. And as for developing a closer relationship with his wife and children — well, he'll work *that* out when he gets his drinking under control. Which, of course, he never will.

What about Ann? Although it may not be obvious on the surface, she gets just as much out of the relationship as Miller does. First of all, she gets to feel good about herself for sticking it out for so many years. "I'm not a saint," she demures, but unconsciously nods her head in agreement.

Ann, who sees herself as The Strong One in the marriage, also gets to feel that she is truly helping her husband. "What would he do without me?" she often thinks. "I'm his only chance." This isn't true, of course — an objective look at the past thirty years would prove that. But Ann can't be objective because she needs to believe she is helping her husband.

Finally, by enmeshing herself in her husband's "problem," Ann can avoid dealing with problems of her own. Every time Miller goes through a crisis, she sees about getting help for *him*. She has often called Alcoholics Anonymous for Miller but she has never once called

Al-Anon for herself, just as she has never sought therapy on her own behalf.

His problem is drinking and my problem is him, Ann thinks. But that's a delusion. Ann's problem is herself. Like her husband, she is living her life *exactly* as she wants to live it. Her protests, her many resolutions to leave, her threats and pleas are only a smoke screen. In Miller, Ann has not only the husband she wants but the husband she needs.

Most of us willingly wallow in our pain awhile, not because we like it, but because its familiarity offers security. We find some comfort in our pain because at least it holds no surprises.

Each Day a New Beginning
September 13

Why Is It So Hard to Change?

To the outside world, people like Miller and Ann seem to be caught in lifestyles that make them unhappy. Time and time again, they seem to make choices they don't want to make.

How crazy, you think. How can people be so self-destructive? Before you get too puffed up, think about something in your own life that you've wanted to change. Maybe it's a major behavior pattern, like Miller's drinking. Or maybe it's only a minor "bad habit." Maybe it's something far less tangible, like being more open and revealing about yourself. You've wanted — and tried — to change, but couldn't. That's only human. Change, in any form, is very difficult.

Why can't we do what we think we *want* to do? Why can't we do what we believe will make us *happy?* One problem is that too often we confuse "happiness" with "comfort." While Miller and Ann aren't happy with their lives, they *are* comfortable with them — just as we (if we are being honest about it) are usually comfortable with our bad habits.

And what about the concept of happiness itself? Miller gives lip service to the idea that he will be happy if only he stops drinking. Subconsciously, he doesn't believe this at all, and for some very good reasons. During his brief bouts of sobriety, Miller has found life dull and boring. He has felt vulnerable to anxiety and insecurity. He has found himself forced to confront many neglected areas of his life. Does this sound like happiness to you? It doesn't to Miller either.

Miller has never acknowledged that being sober entails a number of challenges and responsibilities. These challenges and responsibilities don't offer happiness in themselves. Instead, they offer opportunities to work toward happiness. But Miller doesn't want opportunities — he wants to stop drinking and be instantly happy. When this doesn't happen, he starts drinking again.

On the surface, it seems that Miller's struggle is with alcohol, but this isn't so. His real struggle is with getting close to life and to other people, and that's a struggle most of us can identify with.

Just like Miller, we may sincerely believe we want to become closer to others. We may have convinced ourselves happiness will be ours if only we can be less withholding with ourselves.

But our ventures into reality may have taught us something quite different. We may have found that attempts at openness have left us feeling fearful and vulnerable. If we have made the mistake of getting close to the wrong people, our fears about being misunderstood or taken advantage of may have come true. Unless we have been brave enough to acknowledge that openness doesn't necessarily bring instant happiness, we have probably gone back to our old, withholding position.

We may have forgotten that some risks are healthy. Fear only teaches more fear. We must experience some failure and some pain if we are to grow and learn.

The Promise of a New Day
November 22

People are never masochistic in the pure sense of the word; animal behavior doesn't work that way. At bottom, despite our ambitions to change, we do what we want to do. We do what makes us comfortable.

To change a behavior, we must become willing to experience a certain degree of discomfort. We must be willing to take risks. Most of all, we must be willing to *work* toward happiness and fulfillment. Otherwise, we are likely to remain what we have always been.

Payoffs and Secondary Gains

When we try to change, we don't meet with instant success or instant happiness. Instead, we are likely to experience discomfort and frustration. Needless to say, this doesn't do much to reinforce our desire to change.

Yet there's another piece to the puzzle, one that reinforces our desire to stay the same. That's the issue of payoffs and secondary gains.

A *payoff* is just what the name implies. You do something and you receive a reward, or payoff. Just as a rat will not run a maze without getting a pellet of food for its efforts, so human beings will not do things unless they get something in return.

Because we are not rats, our rewards don't have to be tangible. We don't have to be paid off in food or even in wealth. Instead, we do many things for payoffs that are purely psychological. If we have life scripts which encourage us to be happy, then we will seek positive payoffs. If we have negative life scripts, then we may seek payoffs that are damaging and even self-destructive.

Jerry has a life script that might be titled "Be Alone." Like most of us, he's unaware of this script and the role it plays in his life. Jerry believes he wants to be intimate with people, especially women. He tells himself there is nothing he would like better than being in love and having a close relationship.

And Jerry tries. He rushes out, full of enthusiasm, and finds someone to fall in love with. He tells her everything about himself and invests huge amounts of time, energy, and trust in the relationship.

Jerry does all the right things. Unfortunately, he always manages to do them with the wrong person. The women Jerry falls in love with all have one thing in common: For a variety of reasons, they are incapable of forming an intimate relationship with him. No matter how hard Jerry tries, the relationships don't work. For Jerry, there's a payoff in this behavior. The payoff is that he gets to fulfill his life script. He gets to *Be Alone*.

Another term for payoff is *secondary gain.* Whenever we persist in doing something we don't consciously want to do, we can be sure we are getting a secondary gain from that behavior.

If Miller could stop drinking, he would achieve a primary gain: sobriety. If Miller's wife could leave him, she would achieve a primary gain: freedom. If Jerry could fall in love with a different sort of woman, he would achieve a primary gain: intimacy.

Because Miller, Ann, and Jerry don't change, they fail to achieve primary gains. But they *do* achieve secondary gains. Remember the rewards that kept Miller and Ann married to each other? Miller could drink without guilt, evade the responsibilities of life, and be reasonably

63

sure that Ann, his nurse, would always be there
to pick up the pieces. As for Ann, she could feel
strong and virtuous even while she avoided ex-
amining her own problems. These are good
examples of secondary gains; they are rewards
we are not consciously aware of.

Whenever we want to change our behavior,
we should begin by asking ourselves, "What
do I get out of acting the way I do now?"
Ninety-nine times out of a hundred, the first
answer to this question will be "Nothing." But
this is never the real answer. We get something
out of most self-destructive behaviors. Until we
can come to terms with that, we will not be able
to move toward change.

Getting Better vs. Getting Well

So what is it that one wants? The primary or
the secondary gain? On some level, we want
them both. If I am a self-withholding person, I
may yearn for the joys of love and intimacy. At
the same time, unconsciously, I yearn for the
safety and security of remaining just as I am.

It doesn't take a genius to see that these two
goals are in conflict with each other. The sensi-
ble thing to do would be to pick the most desir-
able goal and work *only* toward it.

Most of us don't do that, however. We don't
do it because we are unaware of our subconscious desires; we never even realize we're trying to achieve two goals at once.

Trying to change and failing, over and over
again, is often a sign we are divided about what
we really want. A classic example of this is the

eating disorder bulimia. The bulimic binges on food then purges it from the system. The disease has to do with why we eat and is actually an attempt to satisfy two conflicting goals: the desire to eat large amounts of food and the desire to remain slender.

Trying to change can be a good sign or it can be a sign that we are not trying to change at all. Moreover, when we try and fail repeatedly, we are creating a dangerous precedent for ourselves — we are programming ourselves to expect failure.

Someone once said there are only two ways to go about self-improvement: You can get better, or you can get well. This isn't to say your first attempt at change will be a success — usually it isn't. Most of us stumble and fall many times before we succeed at anything. We shouldn't blame ourselves for not winning a marathon with our very first step.

We can decide on a reasonable, manageable objective for this 24-hour period. Enough days committed to the completion of enough small objectives will bring us to the attainment of any goal, large or small.

Each Day a New Beginning
August 25

Yet "trying" to change can become a game — a self-deceptive and self-destructive one. Unless we courageously examine our motives, unless we are ready to give up secondary goals for primary ones, unless we are willing to *stop* getting better and *start* getting well — then we are likely to use "trying" as a screen to hide behind. We are likely to live our whole lives under the illusion that we are getting better, when all we are really doing is staying the same.

Withholding is not a trait we are born with. It is a behavior that we learn, and choose, just as we might choose to drink or to gamble. For most of us, the choice is an unconscious one. But that doesn't make it any less a choice.

Everything you have just read about behavior, about change, about payoffs and secondary gains, can be applied to withholding. Like other learned behaviors, withholding has rewards. We maintain a withholding position in life because of the payoffs and secondary gains that position brings us. We may find isolation comfortable, comforting, and safe. The very notion of change may leave us feeling threatened and vulnerable.

To change, we must be ready to examine our motives and goals. We must be willing to *un*learn and *un*choose this particular way of being. Most of all, we must be willing to experience uncertainty and even discomfort as we go about finding a new and better way of being.

Part III:

Emotional Shell Games

We do not
always welcome
change.
Often
the change even seems
to intensify
the pain for a spell.
But, in time we'll
clearly see the need
for the
change.

7

The Games People Play

There are many ways to spend our time on Earth. We can spend it enjoying the company of others, improving ourselves, making the world a better place to live, or developing our skills and talents. Or we can waste our time, plodding along in lockstep, leaving our talents undeveloped, failing to make contact with those around us.

People who are frightened of intimacy waste the precious time allotted them for establishing relationships. They cannot act spontaneously because their fear of revealing themselves inhibits them. To keep themselves safe, they seek refuge in a variety of numbing, even destructive, games.

This chapter is about the games people play — games that keep them from interacting with others in a real and honest way. There are many more games than the ones listed here. You may know someone who plays a game quite different from anything described here. There are as many games and variations on games as there are troubled people who play them.

What marks a way of behavior as a game? Here are a few ways to tell.

- *Games have ulterior motives.* The game player pretends to do one thing while in fact she is doing something quite different.

- *Games are repetitive.* The person who is game-free can act and react in a wide variety of ways. The game-playing person finds himself acting in the same ways over and over again.

- *Games use other people.* The game-playing person does not see others as fully human. She views them as pawns, as opponents, or as spoils to be competed for.

- *Games have payoffs.* People play games because they are looking for a particular gain or payoff. In the case of the games described here, the "payoff" is *successfully avoiding self-disclosure.*

I will describe 22 games, arranged in alphabetical order. Besides describing each game, I also offer a remedy. Although I give suggestions for things to do and things to become aware of, what matters most is the game player himself. Unless he is determined to stop the game, no amount of insight can help.

Games often arise from our life scripts — those messages we have been carrying around since the age of five. It is no wonder, then, that breaking the pattern is so difficult. In fact, it has been compared to trying to change the course of a river. Even the most determined person may need help to bring the change about. This help can come from a professional, from a formal support group, or from the friends and family in one's life. And while a lucky few may be able to accomplish change overnight, the process for most of us is slow going, with many slips and slides before we reach the goal.

The withholding games described in this chapter include:

The Actress

The Game: This game requires a higher degree of emotionalism than most men in our society care to show. They are more likely to use the strategy described in playing Possum. The Actress lives in a state of high drama. Her personal relationships are stormy and tempestuous. So are her relationships at work, where her high-voltage feelings frequently interfere with her ability to get the job done. If she is in therapy, she has many "breakthroughs" but rarely, if ever, achieves lasting progress.

On the surface it seems that the Actress is simply a breed apart; fated to live fast, die young, and "do it all" in between. A closer look reveals that the Actress is very much the author of her own drama. She fills her life with people who are unavailable, abusive, or emotionally unbalanced. She neglects little things (like paying the rent or getting the roof fixed) until disaster results.

The technicolor feelings the Actress professes are essentially phony reactions to the stage business she has set in motion. Her *real* feelings, which she doesn't want to deal with, are carefully hidden beneath her turbulent facade. The Actress suspects her "real" self is not special or lovable. To be loved, she must put on a show and pull people into her drama.

The Actress's life is studded with short-lived, superficial relationships because other people (unless they are playing games themselves) see the falseness of her emotions and pull away from her.

The Remedy: As a child, the Actress may have gotten a lot of attention by throwing tantrums, or she may have seen her parents continually quarreling and making up. For whatever reasons, she decided that larger-than-life emotions are better than life-sized ones.

The Actress must go back, examine this early decision, and make a new decision about life. She must be willing to stop the drama and sweep the stage clean of self-created crises and trumped-up emotions. Then she will be able to experience, accept, and share her real feelings.

The Addict

The Game: Research indicates that addiction to alcohol and other drugs is not simply a psychological problem. Some people are more vulnerable than others because of their biochemical makeup. Yet it is a cop-out to blame one's biology. The Addict has chosen to become a victim of his own biochemistry rather than to protect himself against it.

The Addict is afraid of his own feelings, which he seeks to numb with drugs, alcohol, or both. Because intimacy and feeling go hand in hand, he is also terrified of forming close relationships. To avoid his feelings, the Addict chooses to interact with a chemical substance instead of with people. The high he gets provides the drama and stimulation he would normally get from human beings. Moreover, being high obscures the feelings of emptiness that haunt him.

Because intimate, game-free relationships frighten the Addict, he uses his addiction to manipulate the people in his life. To the Addict, people are either Rescuers or Persecutors — good guys or bad guys. (Usually, they are forced to be both.) People are not free to be themselves around the Addict, and this effectively bars the path to intimacy.

The Addict babies himself and blames himself at the same time. On one hand, he believes he is special: sensitive, gifted, and extraordinarily intelligent. Yet he also fears he is a loser, unlovable, and doomed to fail at whatever he tries. Here again, he is helped out by a chemical high. In an altered state, he manages to feel "okay" about himself, something he never really feels when he is drug-free.

Besides alcohol and other drugs, other popular addictions include food (see the Fat Person) and work (see Tomorrow At Tara).

The Remedy: The first task for the Addict is to recognize and acknowledge the addiction. Then the Addict must begin taking responsibility: Responsibility for his feelings and responsibility for the direction of his life. He must be willing to abstain from chemicals, feel his emotions (even if they are painful, as emotions often are), and he must be willing to give up the illusion that he is unique.

The roles of Rescuer or Persecutor or both, which the Addict forces upon others are, in part, projections of the way he treats himself. By alternately babying and bullying himself, the Addict stays in a constant state of conflict. Before he can make progress, the Addict must make peace among these warring selves.

The Analyst

The Game: Human feelings pose no problem at all for the Analyst. If something can be felt, it can be examined. If it can be examined, then it need not be felt.

Not surprisingly, most Analysts are bright people. They were the kind of children who did well in school and even better in college or in business. One aspect of the Analyst's life is always dim and faulty, however, and that's his social life. While the Analyst is ahead of others in his thinking, he is often at a loss when it comes to loving, having friends, and simply enjoying himself. From a Transactional Analysis point of view, the Analyst is all Adult and no Child.

An intelligent mind is a wonderful thing to have, but the Analyst has used his intelligence to avoid dealing with his feelings. If a wife complains to her Analyst husband that he is cold and undemonstrative, he is likely to respond in a detached way. "What is love?" he asks, turning the question into a philosophical debate.

The Analyst has always earned approval for being "a brain." Secretly, he suspects that giving in to his emotions would turn him into a helpless, quivering mass, a monstrous blob of need that everyone would run away from.

The Remedy: Because the Analyst has always earned approval by *doing* (thinking), he has never learned about the "being" side of nature. Consequently, he's not very good at it. He doesn't really know how to be a friend, a lover, or a partner; he doesn't even know how to be himself.

The Analyst must stop using his intellect to keep people at a distance. He must admit that his needs and feelings are real and important in their own right. His most important task is to let himself *be* more — to let himself play and feel, to allow himself to be spontaneous and vulnerable. When he sees that he can get approval by being himself, the Analyst will no longer need to stifle his emotions.

The Broken Wing

The Game: Broken Wing is a game particularly attractive to women, perhaps because society has often encouraged them to be helpless and dependent. Men can play this game too, although they usually play a harder version of it, becoming addicts and even criminals.

The Broken Wing's life is a real mess. She walks around with her arm in a sling, talking about how tough things are and how it's "just her luck" that things never work out. The Broken Wing's problem isn't sharing her feelings — she carries her lament to anyone who'll listen. Her problem is taking responsibility for those feelings.

The Broken Wing's game goes something like this: She confides in you and her problems become your responsibility. Her own massive needs always come first — she's been wounded, and you're the one who's supposed to fix her up. She is seldom receptive to the needs of others and, therefore, rarely develops healthy intimate relationships.

The amazing thing is that the Broken Wings *do* develop relationships. Female Broken Wings usually pair up with Gurus; male Broken Wings find Nurses to look after them.

The Remedy: The Broken Wing's obsessive "sharing" amounts to nothing more than avoiding responsibility. To her, intimacy means having someone to dump on. She needs to start taking responsibility for her life, her feelings, and the things that happen to her. She needs to start focusing on the giving — rather than on the taking — aspects of intimacy.

The Challenger

The Game: The Challenger is looking for unconditional approval. He wants you to love him in spite of the barriers he puts in your way. Behind his crusty, often unattractive exterior, is a "true" self he's saving for those who prove themselves worthy. Needless to say, the Challenger rarely, if ever, finds anyone who fits this description. Unconditional love is something reserved for infants — a fact the Challenger refuses to acknowledge.

In his mind, the lack of intimacy in his life isn't his fault at all but the fault of those who won't accept him as is — even though "as is" may mean slovenly, dependent, selfish, rebellious, and antisocial. Like Peter Pan, the Challenger is the child who has never grown up. Although he has high expectations of others, he won't allow others to expect anything at all from him. If they do, they immediately become unworthy — a crime punishable by sulks, pouts, and withdrawal.

The Remedy: The Challenger's key task is to see that he *is* the problem. Usually, he's oblivious to this — like a child, he blames others rather than himself for things that have gone wrong. Once he sees the part he plays in erecting barriers that keep others away, he can begin tearing those barriers down.

The Challenger was often overcriticized as a child. A rebel by nature, he adopted this extreme strategy as a means of expressing his anger and frustration. He needs to go back and reexamine this aspect of his life. Is he still acting out his anger? Is he still trying to insulate himself from his critical parents? Realizing that these strategies are no longer necessary or appropriate will help him let go of them.

The Chameleon

The Game: Like nature's chameleon who camouflages itself by changing shades, this person hides from others by shifting ego states. If you are speaking to the Chameleon on an adult-to-adult basis, she will suddenly let the Child part of her personality take control. If you are both in your Child, the Chameleon may shift to her aloof and judgmental Parent.

For example, one partner may say to another, "Sometimes, I'm afraid of making a commitment to you." Instead of sharing similar fears or reassuring her partner of her love, the Chameleon will dance away, making a statement like, "Have you always been so neurotic?"

The Chameleon's continual shifting limits communication and slams the door on intimacy. Usually, the person who is dealing with the Chameleon isn't even sure what has happened — he only knows that he feels frustrated and pushed away.

The Chameleon is just as oblivious to what she's doing as are the people around her. She doesn't consciously think, I'm going to avoid sharing my real self with this person by shifting ego states. The fast switches the Chameleon pulls are unconscious — but that doesn't make them any less effective. By trial and error, the Chameleon has learned that certain types of responses will throw the other person off balance and keep the conversation on a safely superficial level.

Usually, the Chameleon's fear is loss of control. She may not feel she's a bad person, she may have no secrets to hide, but the idea of making unplanned disclosures is threatening to her. It is so threatening, in fact, that she must keep a tight reign on the conversation at all times — even at the cost of true intimacy.

The Remedy: First, the Chameleon needs to become aware of her own tactics. Because she longs for intimacy even as she seeks to avoid it, she may have a sense of loneliness and dissatisfaction. If she finds herself hungering for the kind of "heart-to-heart" communication others seem to have, she must look at — and take responsibility for — her half of the conversation.

The Chameleon needs to spot her own ego shifts. This can be done by tracking her feelings through a conversation. When does she feel anxiety? What does she say next? Anxiety is usually the trigger for her sudden flight. The Chameleon can improve by learning to confront her anxiety rather than running from it.

The Come-on

The Game: The Come-on is a seductive creature, but something of a Venus's-Flytrap when it comes to intimacy. Because he both longs for closeness and fears it, he gives those around him mixed signals. He's good at sporadic, short-term closeness but true intimacy, for him, remains frightening. When things get too close for comfort, he suddenly pulls away.

When is that pressure point reached? That's the problem — even the Come-on himself doesn't know until it happens. Things may seem fine. Then, all of a sudden, alarms go off inside him and he's in full flight, leaving the other person confused and rebuffed.

Although, at times, he may seem to be caring and considerate, the Come-on's approach to human relationships is essentially a selfish one. When he yearns for closeness, he easily pulls people to him. When closeness becomes uncomfortable, he slams the door on their expectations. The Come-on's self-centered point of view keeps him, in the end, alone and isolated.

The Remedy: Like the Chameleon, the Come-on often fears losing control. He needs to examine these feelings when they come up. Are they appropriate to the situation at hand, or are they leftover messages from childhood?

The Come-on also needs to examine his selfish attitude toward others. Because he attracts people easily, he takes them for granted. Often, the loss of a particularly important person in his life will bring him up short. The key to the Come-on's personal growth is learning to see that people are to be valued — not used and disposed of.

The Crazy Person

The Game: The Crazy Person wears a sign that says, "Beware, and do not expect too much of me, for I am fragile." Beneath the cover of this sign, the Crazy Person is free to indulge in all sorts of otherwise objectionable behavior.

By playing fragile, the Crazy Person feels absolved from the responsibilities of intimacy. She feels no need to be honest, open, loving, or giving. She's crazy — as she told you — so what do you expect?

At the same time, her craziness entitles her to get a lot. She is struggling, she is fragile, her needs are enormous, and the game she plays legitimizes her desire to place those needs ahead of anything else.

People who are around the Crazy Person for very long eventually find themselves feeling frustrated and exhausted. The reason: They are doing all the giving and none of the getting. Intimacy can never be a two-way street with the Crazy Person because she sees herself as unequal, unstable, and weak.

The Remedy: In this age of overly intense introspection, the Crazy Person is likely to blow normal fears, angers, and problems out of proportion. She may claim fragility because she fears intimacy, completely losing sight of the fact that everyone else fears intimacy too.

Even when the Crazy Person's problems are legitimate, her game is not. She must stop using her difficulties as an excuse — she must take responsibility for her actions, attitudes, and interactions in the here and now, regardless of what went on in her past.

The Critic

The Game: The Critic has a deep-seated fear of revealing himself to others, although he's seldom aware of this. Often, he believes there's nothing he'd like more. Critic parents long to be closer to their children; single Critics search endlessly for partners; married Critics yearn for an intimacy that, somehow, never comes.

What goes on in the Critic's life to block intimacy? In a word, *criticism.* The Critic is always on a fault-finding mission. His hidden agenda goes something like this: I can't be open with this person because there's something wrong with him; when someone good enough comes along, then I'll be open.

The Critic thinks of himself as superior, the upholder of standards and good taste. In reality, he is often a tedious boor, rigid and judgmental, incapable of the intimacy he believes he wants.

The Remedy: As a child, the Critic may have been severely judged by his parents. His feelings of fundamental unworthiness and inadequacy haunt him through his adult years, making the prospect of self-disclosure a terrifying one.

The Critic needs to work on rethinking this early life decision. Is he really not okay, or is that only the feeling his parents gave him about himself? If the Critic can make the switch — decide he is indeed okay — then he can allow the rest of the world to be okay as well. He will no longer need to hide his flawed and faulty self, and will be able to move toward the intimacy he longs for.

Daddy Warbucks

The Game: Daddy Warbucks has traditionally been a man's game. As women find work outside the home and gain economic power, they become eligible players as well. A few very strong women have played the game without working outside the home, in which case the game is called Matriarch.

Daddy Warbucks is the ultimate provider. It's his labor that puts food on the table, clothes in the closet, and gas in the car. He works so those around him might prosper. But Daddy Warbucks is more than a provider — he's also a despot. As Daddy Warbucks learned long ago, he who controls the purse strings *controls*. Daddy Warbucks is willing to share his cash but not his feelings. Consequently, he uses his role as provider to keep his wife and children at arm's length.

The Remedy: Why is Daddy Warbucks so uncomfortable with feelings? Often, he has a life script that says, "Emotions are weak." This is especially true for men who were encouraged by their parents and by society not to show emotion.

Daddy Warbucks needs to take another look at this life script. He needs to give himself permission to feel — even if that means feeling inadequate, frightened, and vulnerable from time to time.

When he sees that his family will not abandon him for having these feelings, he will no longer need to keep them at such a distance. He can stop using money as a means of achieving love and respect.

The Discounter

The Game: The Discounter devalues the importance of feelings — his own as well as everyone else's. If he feels lonely or isolated, he's likely to shrug his discomfort aside. If a friend confesses to feeling frightened or insecure, he's likely to respond, "So what?"

There are several techniques the Discounter uses. He may simply deny his (or others') feelings completely. Or he may be aware of his feelings but unwilling to "waste time talking about them." Still another approach is to claim that "everyone feels like this" — thus depriving feelings of their special and unique qualities.

The Discounter's game works two ways. First, it keeps him from opening up to others. Second, it discourages others from opening up to him. People who confide in the Discounter often come away feeling wounded and rebuffed; made to feel as if their feelings just don't matter.

The Remedy: Often, the Discounter has a lifescript that says "Don't Feel." (Perhaps this is why so many Discounters, encouraged by cultural stereotypes, are men.) Since all Discounters are human and since all humans feel, the Discounter needs to realize he is trying to live out a script that is impossible. He needs to give himself permission to feel and to realize feelings — his own as well as those of others — are important and essential.

The Entertainer

The Game: Some Entertainers actually take

to the stage as a career, others merely make small stages of their own lives. Either way, the Entertainer is easy to spot: He's the person who can hold an audience in the palm of his hand, spellbinding them with fascinating tales or delighting them with laugh-a-minute jokes.

Because the Entertainer is always at the center of a crowd and because he is almost always doing the talking, he's the last person you'd suspect of withholding himself from others — but that's often just what's going on. If you look closely, you'll see that the Entertainer functions best when he's on stage, setting the pace, with his listeners safely in their chairs. Any member of the audience who breaks this rule and gets too close is likely to be shunned as a heckler.

The Entertainer is great in front of a group. Get him alone, in a one-on-one situation, with an outcome he can't control, and he isn't nearly so comfortable. Putting on a show is comfortable to him; sharing his inner self is not. For this reason, many Entertainers eventually become tragic clowns, laughing on the outside and crying on the inside.

The Remedy: Aside from wanting to demolish the barriers he himself has erected, the Entertainer must also take a hard look at the secondary gains his game brings him. In most cases, his role as Entertainer fosters the illusion that he is exalted, unique, and superior to those in his audience. Before he can comfortably share his feelings with others, the Entertainer must give up this illusion. He must come to see himself and others as equals, partners in the business of living and loving.

85

The Fat Person

The Game: Although the Fat Person is not always a woman, the proportion of women who have some kind of eating disorder is vastly higher than the proportion of men who suffer similar problems.

Many of the statements made about the game played by the Addict (page 73) also apply to the Fat Person. However, the Fat Person's game has an extra component: the layer of armor (fat) she carries as a result of her compulsive eating.

The Fat Person lives on a merry-go-round. At an early age, she has learned to deny her feelings — to literally stuff them down by swallowing large amounts of food. As her behavior leads her further and further into isolation, her feelings of loneliness, anger, and sadness grow, making it necessary to consume even larger amounts of food.

The excess weight that results from overeating is important to the Fat Person. It is, literally, armor against the world. Women often gain weight to keep them safe from men, sex, and intimate relationships. Just as often, weight becomes a scapegoat, the reason the Fat Person never married, failed to achieve career success, or missed pursuing some vital interest.

While the Fat Person bears a strong resemblance to the Addict, she also has a strong streak of the Challenger in her. She longs to be loved and admired just as everyone else does, but insists that others love her in spite of the fact her primary involvement is with food.

The Remedy: The Fat Person must recognize her addiction and stop using her body as a scapegoat. Since overweight people *do* achieve love, success, and happiness, the Fat Person must realize that she — not her body — is responsible for the emptiness in her life.

The Fat Person feels her problem is an insatiable appetite, but this is seldom the case. Her real problem is her resistance to being thin, which fosters her appetite. To the Fat Person, thin means vulnerable, accessible, and being in touch with feelings. When the Fat Person becomes willing to surrender her armor, her need to use food as a replacement for relationships will diminish.

The Fat Person must learn not only to accept her feelings but to allow herself to feel positively about her body. If she can do this, she will learn to nourish rather than stuff herself, thus stopping the abuse that has gone on.

Once she has accepted her body, she can begin forming relationships with others who also accept her. (Previously, the self-hating Fat Person may have surrounded herself with people who reflected her own critical, unloving attitudes.) Forming positive relationships with others will take away the loneliness the Fat Person feels — a gap she has previously tried to fill with food.

The Guru

The Game: The Guru appears in many forms: He may see himself as a savior, spiritual guide, a teacher, therapist, or healer. Yet behind his mask of all-knowingness, the Guru is none of these things. He is not truly concerned with helping, sharing, or caring but with armoring his own insecure ego.

To keep others from seeing how inadequate he is, the Guru must constantly put himself in a superior position. He accomplishes this by convincing himself he is gifted with special wisdom or insight. Certain that he *knows best,* he sets about enlightening those around him — pointing out their flaws, telling them how to live their lives, congratulating himself on the *good work* he's doing.

Often, to make the illusion complete, he surrounds himself with people who are floundering and inadequate — Broken Wings who are in no position to challenge him or reject his brand of salvation. Even if there are no Broken Wings around, the Guru will preach his message *ad nauseum.* If anyone protests or tells him to mind his own business, he's likely to adopt a martyred expression and protest, "But I'm doing this to help you."

The Remedy: The Guru must confront the truth about himself: Instead of caring about others, he uses those around him to bolster his own insecure ego. He must have the courage to admit he doesn't want to see people succeed nearly as much as he wants to assure himself that no one is quite as good as he is. The Guru can learn the true meaning of loving and sharing, but he must drop the illusions he holds about himself: The lie that he is gifted with special knowledge; the tortured belief that he is inadequate. If the Guru can accept and love himself as he is, he'll no longer need to judge others so harshly.

The I Don't Want to Burden You Person

The Game: This is a game most often played by women, who are encouraged to be passive and, as a consequence, feel especially at home in the role of Shrinking Violet.

The I Don't Want To Burden You Person is a natural sidekick, someone who would rather talk about the exploits of others than about herself. When it comes to making friends, she attaches herself to people she sees as more powerful, more intelligent, and more important than she is.

If there's a difference of opinion, the I Don't Want To Burden You Person trusts the other person's intuition, not her own. In fact, she often waits to hear what someone else thinks before going out on a limb to express her own ideas.

As for sharing feelings, she'll listen unflaggingly to other people's tales of woe, always coming forward to offer sympathy, support, or whatever she thinks is needed — even if it's inconvenient for her to do so. But she never shares her feelings in return. She believes her own feelings are too unimportant to inflict on anyone else. She doesn't want to be a drag; she doesn't want to burden others with her mediocre, uninspiring ideas.

While this sounds like ultra-considerate behavior, anyone who has ever befriended the I

Don't Want To Burden You Person knows better. Trying to get a fix on how this person feels is like pulling teeth. In the final analysis, this is a withholding game, one that makes others take responsibility for whatever relationship develops.

The Remedy: The I Don't Want To Burden You Person needs to discover her own feelings before she can share them with others. Often, she is out of touch with how she feels and what she wants because she has made a lifestyle of adapting herself to the desires of others.

After the I Don't Want To Burden You Person sees that she has a *right* to her feelings, she must also see that she has a *responsibility* to share them. She must understand that, in choosing passivity, she has opted for the easy way out — a way that keeps her safe from risk and rejection. If she can become courageous enough to brave these hazards, she can unlock her untapped potential for loving.

The Juggler

The Game: On the surface, the Juggler seems to have no problems at all. With dozens of friends and no empty slots on his calendar, his social life is bursting at the seams. Those who want to get close to the Juggler will have to wait in line for the chance.

And that's just the problem. The Juggler uses people to insulate himself. He keeps a steady stream of them coming and going in his life, ensuring that he will never have time to get too close to anyone.

Although he thinks of himself as open and people-loving, the Juggler fears intimacy. He is secretive and elusive about himself and often feels that people are trying to "pin him down." If the Juggler is single, he goes through partners very quickly, never staying long enough to let a relationship develop. If the Juggler is married, he may cheat his partner by letting too many other people claim his time — co-workers, friends, parents, even other lovers.

It's important not to confuse the Juggler with the healthy person who is simply gregarious. Even the friendliest extrovert has a sense of priorities, reserving large chunks of time and energy for those closest to him. The Juggler has no such priorities. Just the opposite, in fact. When a relationship threatens to become too intimate, that's when the Juggler withdraws completely.

The Remedy: A good place for the Juggler to start is with his relationships to others. How do other people seem to him? Would he describe *most* of the people he meets as needy, insecure, jealous, demanding, or anxious for commitments? If so, the Juggler needs to consider the role he is playing. His need to have no demands placed on him may be skewing his vision. Also, his no-strings behavior may be at fault, breeding insecurity in those around him.

It's a good bet that, for whatever reasons, the Juggler knows very little about intimacy. He doesn't know how to go about getting it and is relatively ignorant of its unique rewards. A good first step for him would be to start setting priorities in his life, learning to invest more time and energy in some people than in others. Learning who to open up to and who to trust is something the Juggler has never mastered, but it's a task he must begin.

The Nurse

The Game: This game, which emphasizes compliance, self-sacrifice, and a mothering attitude, is most frequently played by women. However, men can and do join in at times.

The Nurse spends her life trying to anticipate and fulfill the needs of others. She has a strong urge to rescue people and so surrounds herself with those who will use and exploit her: chemically dependent husbands, delinquent children, whining parents, unappreciative friends.

Because the Nurse makes a point of anticipating the needs of others, she expects others to do the same for her. She will not ask for what she wants but will wait passively, longing for rewards that never come.

After years of service, the Nurse finds herself in a state of emotional starvation. The very people she lavished herself on have fled from her. Angry at being neglected, the Nurse may take one of three routes: She may become a nagging martyr, she may become even more passive and withdrawn, or she may begin the cycle all over again, looking for new people to spend herself on.

The Remedy: The Nurse needs to take a close look at the payoffs of her game. By playing caretaker, she gets to feel needed and important. Since none of her relationships are equal ones, she need never disclose herself.

Her own problems remain snugly hidden, even from herself.

The Nurse also needs to examine the nature of her rescuing. Is she really helping others, or is she simply aiding and abetting their difficulties? Caring for people is fine, but smothering them is something else. Part of the Nurse's game may be to bind people to her by keeping them needy and dependent. Flight is their only escape, which explains why the Nurse so often finds herself alone and abandoned.

The Nurse's major task lies in getting in touch with herself — her own problems, her own needs. She must start asking for what she wants, rather than foisting that responsibility upon others. If there is a major problem in her life, she must tackle it head on, rather than expect it to disappear while she is off rescuing someone else.

The Possum

The Game: Like the animal for whom this game was named, the Possum has a unique ability to play dead. He appears to have no feelings at all, and is so convincing he often fools himself as well as others. The Possum can be either a man or a woman, although society, with its emphasis on male stoicism, does more to encourage men in this game.

The Possum holds firm with the belief that, to get through life, you've got to be tough. This means cutting himself off from his feelings. To the Possum, feelings are merely chinks in the armor, signs of weakness and vulnerability.

Thus he goes through life stifling his joy and anger.

Because he is locked up emotionally, the Possum often comes across as cold or distant. He is never able to share, as other people do, this large and important part of himself. Because he is out of touch with his emotions, he is unable to learn from them. While those around him grow and change, the Possum is frozen in place.

Since suppressed emotions take their toll on the body, the Possum is susceptible to any number of physical ills. He may grind his teeth, develop high blood pressure, have migraine headaches, or suffer from tense, painfully aching muscles. Even these warning signs do not alert the Possum, whose impulse is to ignore what's going on inside him and keep struggling, as best he can, with the outside world.

The Remedy: The Possum who wishes to change must look at his original life script. What made him decide feelings are dangerous? How did this decision become a permanent philosophy of life?

Often, the Possum had parents who ridiculed or otherwise punished him for revealing his feelings. This nonphysical yet nevertheless brutal abuse, suffered at the hands of those whose approval he wanted most, led the Possum to regard his feelings as weapons that could be used against him. The Possum learned not only to withhold his feelings but to "disarm" himself by pretending feelings simply didn't exist.

For the Possum, healing comes in small doses. His first step is to explore his own emotional terrain. While this is second nature for most of us, the Possum must make a special effort. He must ask himself whether he feels mad, sad, glad, or afraid about things.

The Possum's second task — sharing his feelings with others — is just as important. He must find those who will reward him for having feelings, rather than punish him as his parents did. As he receives positive reinforcement from himself and those around him, the Possum will be able to formulate a more rational life script, one which says feelings are okay.

The Proxy

The Game: Although men can play this game, it seems to come more easily to women, who generally have a larger support network to draw on.

The Proxy has mastered the art of confession. Frequently, she has schooled herself on magazine articles, pop psychology books, and radio psychology until she has the lingo down pat. She can describe any problem or emotion in just the right terms, and is likely to strike others as remarkably insightful.

The trouble is that the Proxy misapplies what she has learned. If she is having a problem with her partner, she makes no disclosures to him but goes instead to a proxy, a disinterested third party who is not involved in the situation. Her efforts are aimed in the wrong direction: She makes intimate disclosures to drive a wedge between herself and those she loves most. By the time she has discussed her feelings with half a dozen other people, she seldom has the energy or the incentive left to share her feelings with those who truly count in her life.

The Remedy: Much of the Proxy's behavior is simply a bad habit. It's easier to share ourselves with people who have no stake in our lives because, in doing so, we risk nothing. The Proxy has simply learned to take the easy way out, and this has become a destructive habit, one with consequences she should take time to consider.

The Proxy also needs to think about the fact that she may be playing a game called "Good Guy, Bad Guy." Does she disclose the full story, or does she paint a scene in which she is eternally good, wise, and well-meaning while her partner is selfish, stupid, and immature?

The wonderful thing about confiding in a third party is that you won't get any arguments — as the Proxy well knows. Thus, her seeming disclosures may be nothing more than crying sessions, effective only for whipping up her already well-developed sense of self-pity. To break her pattern, the Proxy must be willing to stop complaining and risk being challenged.

The Right Stuff Person

The Game: The Right Stuff Person hides behind a wall of material possessions. His life is lived according to trend, and he has refined consumerism to an art: His apartment is full of the latest electronic toys, his closet is bursting with stylish clothes, his conversation is studded with references to celebrities in the news. If the

Right Stuff Person is a woman, an extra layer of camouflage is added in the form of makeup, which she has spent years learning to apply.

Some find conversation with the Right Stuff Person boring, others find it fascinating. The Right Stuff Person is a faithful reporter. He knows what's hot and what's not, has seen all the new movies and read all the right books, and can be counted on to keep his listeners informed.

But the Right Stuff Person's conversation, like his life, is all outer-directed. He never talks about his own feelings or ventures to share an original idea. After a while, this becomes a limitation and people seeking more than superficial reportage pull away from him. Right Stuff women often marry Right Stuff men and drift for years in hollow, unsatisfying marriages.

The Right Stuff Person needs this elaborate costuming because he feels that he is not worth noticing. He believes his feelings are banal and boring; not nearly as exciting as the feelings of the rich, famous, and talented. In the Right Stuff Person's mind, it's always better to be a good imitation rather than a poor original.

The Remedy: The Right Stuff Person labors under the belief that he can literally become what he buys. Acquiring things gives him an illusory sense of power and importance, and surrounding himself with them makes him feel secure.

The Right Stuff Person needs to confront this illusion head-on. He needs to consider the fact that frantic collecting is an attempt to fill up the hollow spots in his life. Because the Right Stuff

Person has spent so much time acquiring and absorbing, he has neglected other aspects of his life. Usually, his personal relationships are shallow and unsatisfying; he seldom gets from them the reassurance he desires. Frequently, his career life is also a disappointment, since he has never stretched himself to develop his talents.

The Right Stuff Person needs to throw away his props (or at least push them off stage for awhile) and work on presenting himself as is. Since he may have surrounded himself with a crowd of other Right Stuff people, he may have to change his friends to do so. However, many other people will give him positive reinforcement for being himself — exactly what the Right Stuff Person needs to begin filling the yawning gaps in his self-image.

The Skin-Deep Person

The Game: Because of the high priority placed on feminine beauty in most cultures, this game is commonly played by women, but men can play as well.

The Skin-Deep Person is physically attractive, although she often doesn't think so. To make up for her "flaws," she spends a lot of time working on her exterior. If she puts up a good front, the Skin-Deep Person thinks people won't see how shallow and unattractive she really is.

Is the Skin-Deep Person really shallow? She often ends up that way. Focusing on her physical appearance leaves little time for self-improvement. She can get by on her looks and has no scruples about taking advantage of the situation. Because of this, she has not learned to cooperate with others or to share herself with them. She lacks the basic understanding needed to build sound relationships.

This brings a lot of sadness into the Skin-Deep Person's life. She often complains of being treated like an object. "I want to be loved for myself," she cries. But the game she plays keeps that from happening. She sees herself only as an object. She polishes her exterior and ignores her inner self, and she usually attracts people who treat her the same way. The meager love the Skin-Deep Person receives doesn't make her happy. Anyone who is too stupid to see past her glitzy exterior is a fool in her eyes. She believes the only people whose love is worth having are those who are wise enough to see through her and reject her.

The Remedy: The Skin-Deep Person uses physical attractiveness as armor — armor she has adopted because she is frightened of letting others get close to her. To be loved "for herself," as the Skin-Deep Person longs to be, she must stop regarding herself as an object. She must stop trading on her good looks, and must accept her real or imagined physical flaws. Most of all, she must begin learning the lessons she has thus far avoided: cooperation and sharing, giving to others as opposed to merely taking from them.

The Tomorrow At Tara Person

The Game: Rhett, Ashley, and saving Tara from the Yankees, kept Scarlett O'Hara awfully busy. So busy, in fact, that she seldom had time to feel. Whenever a twinge of discomfort assaulted her, she'd push it aside. "I'll think about that tomorrow," she told herself; "tomorrow at Tara there'll be time for that."

Not surprisingly, tomorrow never came. Scarlett kept pushing her feelings aside, realizing she loved Rhett only when he lost patience and walked out on her.

Like Scarlett, the Tomorrow At Tara Person often realizes his feelings too late. On a day-to-day basis, he keeps himself so busy there is no time left for his emotions. Do, do, do is the order of the day, and the Tomorrow At Tara Person is frequently a high achiever who wins admiration for his many accomplishments.

In spite of these accomplishments, the Tomorrow At Tara Person is seldom truly happy. He has left too many emotions untended. His hard-driving nature may have driven loved ones away from him, leaving him alone or trapped in brittle, impersonal relationships. Realization often comes only when he loses something or someone of value to him.

Because he has ignored his feelings, the Tomorrow At Tara Person is often filled with regret. *If only I had enjoyed my youth. If only I had spent more time with my children. If only I knew you loved me!* These are the kinds of remorseful thoughts the Tomorrow At Tara Person frequently lives with.

In the past, the Tomorrow At Tara Person was likely to be a man. Today, with the explosion of women into the work force, it's just as likely to be a woman. As one psychologist has pointed out, the modern woman may successfully avoid intimate relationships by being "otherwise engaged," caught up in her career and unavailable to men.[1]

The Remedy: As a child, the Tomorrow At Tara Person probably got lots of reinforcement for doing things. At the same time, he may have gotten no reinforcement at all (or even negative reinforcement) for simply being himself. As a result, this person decided he was fundamentally unworthy, acceptable only when he got things done.

The Tomorrow At Tara Person needs to reexamine this early life decision. He needs to spend less time *doing* and more time *being.* This isn't easy. In fact, it flies in the face of all the Tomorrow At Tara Person believes. If he stops doing, then he'll become nothing at all. Even worse, the feelings he has been pushing aside will come bubbling to the surface.

Nevertheless, if the Tomorrow At Tara Person can give himself permission to simply exist — as well as permission to feel troubled, sad, and vulnerable — he will discover the delights and joys hidden in his disowned self.

Our
emotional health
is proportionate
to the freedom
with which
we
willingly share
ourselves
with the people
close to us.

8

The Gifts of Openness

Is there something about yourself you've never shared with anyone else? Are there topics you shy away from because they strike too close to home? Do you go around feeling like a fraud, dreading the day when you'll unwittingly give yourself away?

Imagine, for a moment, that these terrible secrets — the ones you have spent much of your life protecting — have been made known to others. And Imagine that, instead of being rejected, persecuted, or abandoned, you have been rewarded with love and acceptance.

How do you feel now? Relieved? Freed? Charged with new energy?

Until we can imagine casting off our burdens, it Is difficult to see how they tie us down and hold us back. We plod on year after year, certain that this is how life was meant to be for us.

The self-withholder believes that who she is, not what she does, keeps her in isolation. Yet this is erroneous, for it is the *act* of withholding that does the real damage. When we withhold our thoughts, feelings, and experiences from others, we dig a moat around ourselves — a moat keeps us alone and isolated, unable to lay claim to the gifts of openness that would otherwise be ours.

If we have developed a life-long posture of self-withholding, chances are we do not know what we are missing. What are the gifts of openness? What impact are they likely to have on our lives? Are they worth changing for? Since change requires dedicated work, it's helpful to take a moment to think about what we are working for.

The Mind-Body Connection

Sigmund Freud did not set out to become a psychoanalyst — psychotherapy did not exist at the time. Instead, he began as a medical student and, in the course of his studies, learned many of the body's ills had psychological causes. Freud's lifelong work was to find a psychological way of treating these ills. Eventually, working in the footsteps of a colleague, Joseph Breuer, he discovered that when a patient could share the painful but suppressed and unadmitted incidents of his past, his symptoms often vanished.

Freud's method of treatment, which we know today as *therapy* or *analysis,* was originally called the *talking cure,* for the simple reason that by talking — disclosing oneself — the patient could be cured.

There is a strong connection between the mind and the body, and when the mind seeks to bottle up an inner truth, the body is unquestionably affected. The long-term stress of suppressing one's inner nature may take its toll in any number of ways: high blood pressure, a faltering immune system, tense and rigid muscles, chronic exhaustion and fatigue; and a craving for alcohol or other drugs, food, or cigarettes.

The self-disclosing person does not need to bottle himself up. He does not live in a "red alert" state, tense and waiting. As a consequence, his body is free to expand and relax, to stretch, flex, and play. Because there is an absence of anxiety, the body does not need to be numbed with drugs or alcohol. Energy is not drained by the enormous demands of secret-keeping, and the self-disclosing person finds in his body a strong and supportive ally.

Our shameful acts are not unique, and this discovery is our gift when we risk exposure.

Each Day a New Beginning
June 20

Intimacy, The Two-way Street

Anthropologists tell us waving is among the most ancient of human gestures. By showing an open palm, one stranger shows another she is unarmed and vulnerable — and therefore safe to approach.

Self-disclosure works in much the same way. At the outset, all humans are unknown to each other — they are mysterious others, people who talk and move and act around us but about whom we know little. We may learn something about them by observing their actions, but until they invite us to know them, we are likely to regard them with suspicion and even fear.

105

When one person shares something about herself with another, she makes herself less mysterious and, therefore, less threatening. Her openness shows vulnerability, just as a weaponless palm does. Think of a time in your own life when a stranger won you over by sharing a confidence that suddenly drew the two of you together. Didn't you find yourself relaxing, letting down your guard, and warming up to her?

Intimacy between people is always a two-way street. A relationship grows by the exchange of confidences — small ones at first, but progressively larger and more significant ones as the relationship deepens and grows. Disclosure invites disclosure, while the person who is unwilling to reveal herself to others will find others equally unwilling to reveal themselves to her.

The self-disclosing person does not lie in painful isolation, nor is her life marked by dissatisfying, transient, and superficial friends. Instead, her openness fosters the kind of stable and enduring relationships that enrich the fabric and texture of life.

The Stroke Economy

Although our requirements vary, each and every one of us needs *some* degree of human contact. The simple greeting of "Hello, how are you? That's a beautiful dress you're wearing," contributes something important to our lives, something we can only get from other people.

Eric Berne[1] called these contributions *strokes.* A stroke can be small — a postcard or a phone call — or large — a declaration of love or a testimonial dinner. Not all of us need as many strokes as others to be happy, but none of us can thrive in a strokeless environment.

Of course, to receive strokes you must also give them. And, generally, the more strokes you give, the more you will receive. The person who withholds himself is not good at giving strokes. So much of his time and energy are spent protecting his inner self that he has little left to give others. He is rigid and fearful, afraid any overture on his part will invite a prying response. This person receives few strokes — a tragedy, for strokes are exactly what he needs to counterbalance his feelings of shame, inadequacy, and unlovableness. When a person's stroke hunger is not satisfied, he tries to fill the deficit himself — usually with alcohol or other drugs, food, overwork, or destructive and manipulative games.

The person who is not locked into a withholding position is free to give strokes and to receive them. His stroke economy runs at a surplus, supplying him with a constant source of nourishment. Unlike the stroke-starved withholder, he does not need to manipulate others into giving him strokes, nor does he appeal to artificial substances to fill the void.

The secrets we keep, keep us from the health we deserve.

Each Day a New Beginning
April 10

Knowing Oneself

The withholding person believes she knows herself better than anyone else does. In fact, she thinks she knows herself far better than she would like to. In truth, the withholding person doesn't know herself at all.

Self-disclosure is not just a means by which others know us — it is also a means by which we know ourselves. Other people provide helpful information to us about ourselves. Quite often, they can see things we are blind to. This will not be true of everyone in our lives, of course, but all healthy people have at least one or two people who fill this role.

Yet, self-disclosure does more than elicit feedback from others — it also elicits feedback from the self. When one person shares herself with another, she sees herself in a different light. She experiences a dimension of herself that can be experienced in no other way. That is why it is impossible for the withholding person to truly know herself.

The person who reveals herself to others forms a full and accurate picture of herself. This knowledge helps her direct her life and meet her needs far more successfully than the person whose self-image is inaccurate and incomplete.

Freedom to Be, Freedom to Grow

The most important gift of openness is freedom. The withholding person lives in bondage, a slave to his own need for secrecy. Keeping his true self hidden from others is his chief priority, one that consumes an inordinate amount of time and energy. By building walls around himself, the withholding person has made himself a prisoner. He has limited his options and barred the pathway to spiritual and psychological growth. Moreover, the withholding person has denied himself permission to simply *be* himself. His need to conceal his inner self is a denial of that self, a way of saying "I am not acceptable as I am."

The open person, on the other hand, has given himself full permission to *be*. Because of this, he is free to spend his time and energy as he wishes: building relationships, mastering new skills, setting goals and achieving them. He is not psychologically stuck in the past, and so is free to learn the lessons of the here and now. His spirit can move forward, ripening and maturing with each new experience.

Though seldom remembered, one of the greatest tributes we can give one another is full expression of who we were, who we are, and who we hope to become.

The Love Book
p. 9

109

By the thoughts we
choose to cultivate
and encourage, we
author our experiences
and character. The
failures and successes
in our lives are merely
the effects of our de-
structive or construc-
tive thoughts.
Harmonious and loving
attitudes bring peace
and joy, inharmonious
and fear-filled attitudes
result in pain and conflict.

9

Changing the Script

The life script — the set of inner directives by which each and every one of us operates — has many parts to it. People who are self-withholding have scripts burdened with negative, isolating messages.

- Don't be close.
- Don't trust.
- Don't belong.
- Don't feel.
- Don't love yourself.
- Don't be loved.
- Don't be you.

No adult would accept such commands or respond to them, but as children we are helpless. We accept even the most absurd and destructive messages as gospel, simply because they are handed down to us. Before we know it, we have woven our entire lives around them.

If we have been lucky enough to receive positive messages we can live quite happily by the script we wrote in our early years. But if our script is a negative one, it is up to us to change it.

Reread the last sentence of the last paragraph again, this time in a more personal way. *If my script is a negative one, it is up to me to change it.*

Too many people never get this far. They spend years in analysis or self-analysis identifying the causes of their problems. They feel a great sense of relief when their problems can be traced back to Bad Parents, Bad Luck, or a Bad World. These are people who will never get well, although they'll spend a lot of time thinking they're getting better. For them, self-improvement is simply an elaborate game of Who Done It To Me.

None of us can change until we accept full responsibility for who we are today. Tracing our problems back to their source is *only* helpful if it provides information we can use. It is truly amazing how many people fall under the spell of magical thinking on this point. They truly believe that by assessing blame and apportioning it out they can solve their problems.

This just isn't true. The problems you have today are the result of how you act today, and how you act today is something only you can change.

Looking for scapegoats for our current situation won't get us out of our ruts, it will only mire us deeper. To get free, we need to use our talents and wisdom to good benefit.

Night Light
June 24

As a child, you did not have the power to rationally assess the messages you received from your parents. You have that power now, however. Today you can use that power to begin changing your life script.

Changing a life script is a very difficult matter. To realize how difficult it is, just look at all the people who *want* to change but can never quite manage to do it. That doesn't mean it's impossible, though. If you *allow* yourself to change, it can be remarkably easy. People who remain stuck in one place usually do so for one reason: *Because their desire to stay the same is stronger than their desire to change.*

It is important right now to assess your own desire to redirect your life. Do you really want to, or do you simply "wish" things were different? If you are not ready to change, then expecting miracles of transformation will only make you feel frustrated and inadequate. Read this book knowing that the results for you, at this time, will not be the same as they might be for others.

If, however, you are ready to give up your withholding self, acknowledge the new decision you have made about your life. Some therapists suggest commemorating such new decisions with a written contract or statement. If the idea appeals to you, take as much time and paper as you wish to put your thoughts in writing. Self-to-self contracts typically include resolutions (I want to be more open, more giving of myself, etc.) and a list of prospective gains (to experience less anxiety, to be closer to my children, and so on). During the process of change, such contracts can be powerful sources of inspiration.

If you do not feel comfortable putting your thoughts on paper in this way, it's important to commemorate your new decision in some other way — a way that's comfortable and meaningful to you. You might think of a simple statement that paraphrases your goal, such as, "I was meant to be open and loving" or, "I am okay in spite of my faults." These kinds of phrases, often referred to as *affirmations,* counterbalance and — if repeated often enough — eventually replace the negative messages you are battling against.

Just as we give a coloring book and crayons to a child, so can we give ourselves a palette of beautiful colors with which to paint ourselves.

Night Light
October 4

In the next chapters, you will find seven steps designed to help you become a more open person. Briefly, these steps are:

1. Becoming aware
2. Becoming willing
3. Learning to forgive
4. Accepting yourself
5. Assuming risk
6. Learning to disclose
7. Moving ahead

Each of these steps has something specific to offer, although they are by no means the last word on change. How you achieve change is a very individual matter — as individual as you are. In the course of reading these pages, you may come up with additional steps of your own, steps which are especially meaningful and helpful for you. Wonderful! The important thing isn't to take the actions *I* suggest, but to take actions — whatever they may be — that will bring you to your goal.

When
we understand
ourselves better,
we can move
beyond the past
and walk
towards the future
with surer,
safer steps.

10

Becoming Aware

People come in two types: Those who think they know themselves and those who think they want to know themselves. Each type is likely to be wrong to one extent or another, for very, very few of us ever get to know ourselves fully and completely.

Often, self-awareness is partial and fragmentary. Some parts of the self may be sharply in focus while other parts are blurred and indistinct. We may be quite comfortable with our minds, for example, but cut off from our bodies. Or we may be in tune with our bodies but unaware of the influence our emotions have on them.

And, at the same time we yearn for a deeper understanding of the self, we also dread knowing exactly who that self really is. Many of us imagine that the self hidden within us is monstrous: A crazy, selfish, and demanding demon who will drive others away. Or we fear we will discover a self that is truly special and wonderful.

Why, you ask, would anyone be afraid of finding a wonderful self beneath her workaday exterior? Because *specialness* and *wonderfulness* are awe-inspiring — even frightening — qualities. If we are special and wonderful, then we must give up our excuses once and for all. We must stop indulging in fantasy games like "If Only" and "Maybe Someday." We must stop blaming and start living — a difficult task by anyone's standards.

How, then, can we overcome our blind spots and discover who we really are? In my own life, the people around me have been an enormous help. Different friends, at different times in my life, have pointed out the same flaws in my character, flaws I was unaware of.

Friends have also helped me set aside negative beliefs I've had about myself. For much of my life, I saw myself as a selfish and uncaring person. This was part of my life script, a message I'd received over and over about myself from my parents. Only when my friends pointed out, patiently and persistently, that this wasn't true, was I free to acknowledge — and support — the caring and generous side of my nature.

I believe there is another way to increase one's self-awareness, a way that relies not on feedback from others but on feedback from the self.

All of us have recurring themes in our lives. We may be repeatedly happy in love or repeatedly unhappy in it. We may find career success elusive time after time, or we may triumph in spite of setbacks. Why is life so different for one person than it is for another?

Undoubtedly, we are all born with differing sets of advantages and disadvantages. Some of us will have to struggle fiercely to overcome handicaps, while others will seem to stumble onto good fortune without effort. But these differing circumstances, challenging as they are, do not ultimately determine our happiness or our unhappiness, our success or our failure.

Today our lives can be filled with safety, security, and harmony, if we see and face real dangers and not imaginary ones.

Night Light
August 9

Every individual is the author of his own fate. If a person is repeatedly frustrated or disappointed in one area of life, then he is probably doing something to foster that disappointment. However unwittingly, he is opting for situations and ways of acting that keep him in a losing position.

I know a woman named Barbara who repeatedly complains that her three adult children will not confide in her. Has she been singled out by fate to squander her affection on three uniquely selfish children? Possibly, but because I know both Barbara and her children, I know this isn't so. On those rare occasions when Barbara's children do confide in her, she reacts in a harsh and judgmental way, lecturing them about the mistakes they've made and telling them how to clean up the mess they've created.

Barbara feels cheated and deprived. Like most of us, she looks outside herself to see who, exactly, is cheating and depriving her. What she needs to do instead is look inward, to see how she is cheating and depriving herself.

She needs to examine the part of herself that's responsible for receiving and nurturing confidences. If she can do this, she'll be able to understand — and eventually change — her own role in the drama.

You can discover your own losing behavior patterns by taking a close look at your life. Do you feel disappointed in the way things have worked out for you? Is there one area of life with which you're always dissatisfied? What needs do you have that aren't being met? Identifying the failed parts of your life can help you identify the failing parts of yourself, parts you are currently blind to.

Many people have a hard time looking beyond day-to-day situations to see the larger patterns at work. They can't tell you *where* it hurts, they can only tell you *that* it hurts. Instead of saying, "Here is a need that isn't being met," they suffer along with a vague sense that something important is missing.

According to psychologist Abraham Maslow,[1] there are five basic kinds of human needs: biological needs, the need to feel secure, the need to be accepted, the need for self-esteem, and the need for self-actualization. One way to get in touch with your unmet needs is to let the feeling, sensitive Child inside of you consider each of the following statements.

1. As I grew up, my bodily needs — for food, shelter, clothing and so on — were met. (The need for biological survival.)
2. I grew up with people who made me feel safe and protected. (The need to feel secure.)

120

3. As a child, I felt that I was loved and that I belonged. (The need to be accepted.)
4. My parents and the other people around me let me know that I was okay. (The need for self-esteem.)
5. Even as a child, I was treated as a responsible, capable person. (The need for self-actualization.)

If one of these statements triggers a cry of pain or outrage, you have bumped up against an unmet need, a need you have *learned* (from your parents or from the world around you) not to fulfill.

Right now, as you are reading this, focus on one of these incomplete areas of your life. Just thinking of this *missing link* will probably fill you with anger, sadness, or both. That's perfectly okay.

Chances are you have done this many times before. And chances are when feelings of sadness or anger arose, you looked outside yourself for someone to blame. That's an absolutely human reaction. Anger and sadness are such uncomfortable feelings that we try to get rid of them by transferring them to the outside world. We blame our friends for misunderstanding us, our children for disappointing us, our boss for stealing our glory, and the world for failing to live up to our expectations.

This time, resist the impulse to blame anyone at all. Don't even blame yourself. Instead, look at your actions. Can you see *how* you're keeping your needs from being met? Is there something you do over and over again, something that keeps you in a losing position?

If you can identify even a few of these losing behavior patterns, you have significantly increased your self-awareness.

There are very likable people inside us that struggle to change and become better. We deserve to like ourselves for who we are and who we're becoming.

Night Light
July 28

We need to
KEEP IT SIMPLE
as we change
ourselves.
We need to start
slowly. If we imagine
ourselves as a big
puzzle with many
pieces, we may under-
stand we can only see
our whole selves by
joining together
one piece at a time.

11

Becoming Willing

Wouldn't it be wonderful if we could make our problems disappear just by becoming aware of them? Lots of people think that's exactly what will happen. They spend thousands of dollars and years of time searching for insight into their difficulties, only to discover that insight alone accomplishes nothing.

Change isn't something that "just happens." It's something we must *make* happen, and that takes hard work, persistence, and courage.

Why is it so difficult to change? That question has puzzled students of human behavior for centuries. Freud, as he formed his concepts of psychology, even gave the baffling phenomenon a name. He called it *resistance.*

All of us have a certain amount of resistance. Trying to alter even a small habit, like leaving the cap off the toothpaste, is likely to meet with *some* resistance, while trying to make a major alteration, like becoming more open about ourselves, is going to summon up a very large block of resistance.

There are many ways in which people express resistance. One of the most common is the "Yes, but" syndrome. Have you ever been asked for advice, only to have your suggestions turned aside with statements that began, "Yes, that's a good idea, but. . . ."?

The Yes-but person hides behind an endless barrage of excuses. She wants to change *but* there's always a reason why a particular plan of action won't work for her. Each time she says "Yes, but" she is crushed beneath the stubborn rock of her own resistance.

Another expression of resistance is, "I try but it never works." The person who makes this statement is indulging in fantasy thinking. She believes an evil outside force — *it* — is keeping change from happening. The truth is, there is no magical *it*. There is only the individual and her desire — or refusal — to change.

Other forms of resistance are "I can't" and "I don't know how." People use these statements to avoid taking responsibility. They see themselves as weak and helpless, incapable of change and, therefore, free from having to try.

Knowing *how* people resist change still doesn't explain *why* they resist change. They know they want to change, they may even know what they have to do to make the change happen — yet time after time, they find themselves acting in just the opposite way.

Eric Berne[1] called this "spellbound" behavior, not because he believed in the power of magic but because he believed in the power of life scripts.

All of us are spellbound in a sense. The messages we received from our parents during childhood influenced us to accept certain beliefs as true. Spellbinding messages can be either positive (charms) or negative (curses). One of the charms I received from my parents was the belief I was intelligent, hard-working, and persistent. That belief has been my magic armor in many situations, helping me triumph over difficulties and overcoming obstacles that would otherwise have defeated me.

Far more damaging are curses — spellbinding messages that undermine esteem and self-confidence. The person who avoids self-disclosure, wishes to change but cannot, and may be spellbound by messages like *Don't be close, Don't be loved,* or *Don't be you.* She can't change because, according to her life script, she isn't *supposed* to.

As we grow up, these curses are incorporated into the Parent part of the personality. Since ignoring them would mean not only going against our parents but going against part of the self as well, It's easy to see why breaking free is so difficult.

Even so, this isn't all there is to resistance. No matter how strong a spell is, we wouldn't continue to believe in it unless we got something out of it. Often, that "something" is nothing more than the comfort of following old, familiar behavior patterns. Sometimes, however, the payoff is more considerable: dodging responsibility, winning sympathy, avoiding the unknown, or eluding discomfort. These payoffs, also known as secondary gains, have already been discussed in Chapter Six. I mention them again here because they play such a major role in resistance to change.

Still another piece of the resistance puzzle is basic, old-fashioned fear. We remain stuck in one place because we are afraid of facing an unknown future. (This theme is explored in more detail in Chapter 14: Assuming Risk.)

> *To make the changes we want, we need to let go of unhealthy but comfortable patterns that we're stuck in, the way the trees let their colors change, and finally let go of their leaves altogether.*

Today's Gift
March 1

The person who has not confronted his own resistance is not yet willing to change. He will remain caught in a trap, wanting to be different but unable to overcome his own inner road-blocks.

Changing is something you must choose to do. In order to be successful in that choice, you must summon a generous dose of courage from within. Rollo May once wrote a book called *The Courage To Create.*[2] Because of the title, many people think the book is only for artists. Actually, it is for anyone who struggles to create something new and meaningful, be it a new art form or a new self. In the book, May points out that courage doesn't mean moving ahead without fear or doubt. It means moving ahead *in spite of* fear or doubt. That is what becoming willing is all about — overriding your own misgivings.

Here are some specific ways to keep those misgivings from getting the upper hand.

First, look at the way you express resistance. Are you a "Yes, but" or a "Magical It" person?

Do you rely on statements like "I Can't" and "I Don't Know How"? You can weaken your resistance either by getting rid of these statements or forcing yourself to rephrase them. Instead of saying "Yes, that's a good idea, *but* it won't work for me," say "Yes, that's a good idea *and I will try it even though I believe* it won't work for me." Don't allow yourself to indulge in "Magical It" expressions, either. Instead of saying, "I try but *it* never works for me," say "I try but *I* haven't made it work yet." The word *yet* can be a powerful ally in overcoming your resistance. If you learn to say "I can't *yet*" and "I don't know how *yet*" instead of "I can't" and "I don't know how," you imply that at some point in the future you *can* and *will* achieve your goals.

Second, recognize any spellbinding curses that were placed on you during childhood. Realize only you can break the spell and give yourself permission to do so. After you have done this, ask the powerful Parent within you to invent a new and healthy message to live by, one that will be a charm instead of a curse. If you were cursed with a "Don't be close" message, for example, you might replace it with a message that says "You were meant to give affection and be close to others." Write this message down or commit it to memory. The more often you repeat it, the more firmly embedded in your mind it will become.

Third, identify your secondary gains. (Your hidden payoffs.) This calls for a high degree of honesty, since the motives we come up with are usually anything but flattering. Once you have acknowledged what you are getting out of *not changing,* ask yourself if you are ready to give up those payoffs. If you aren't, there's no point in going on. You will only make yourself miserable — and reinforce your sense of shame and inadequacy — by trying to change and failing. Instead, work on making yourself less dependent on your particular set of secondary gains.

Fourth, make peace with your fear and discomfort. Instead of doing battle with them or expecting them to disappear, accept them as part of the process of change. Realize they're like a bad cold — miserable — but hardly lifethreatening. Remind yourself that in return for putting up with them, you will receive something wonderful and valuable in return.

We can't make much progress toward serenity of the spirit without reconciling the past. If old wounds or conflicts rankle, we need to accept them, forgive them, and let them go. Above all, let's forgive ourselves.

The Promise of a New Day
October 30

12

Learning to Forgive

None of us escapes the pain of being hurt by others at some point in our lives. Some hurts are minor and easily forgotten. Other hurts, however, are so deep they leave permanent scars.

This is especially true of the hurts we received as children. Certain words and actions wound us so deeply that we develop layer upon layer of psychological scar tissue.

The withholding person is often someone who has received such wounds. A variety of negative messages (Don't be close, Don't be you, and so on), have made her afraid to reveal herself. To this person, self-disclosure means rejection, punishment, and betrayal of trust.

The problem with the secretive, self-withholding person is that she has never forgiven the wounds of the past. In a wonderful little book called *Love Is Letting Go of Fear,* Dr. Gerald Jampolsky contrasts forgiving and unforgiving minds. The unforgiving mind, he says, sees the future as a repetition of the past and lacks the ability to change. Rigid and fearful, it sees people and events in certain preconceived ways — ways that enforce negative assumptions and beliefs.[1]

The forgiving mind, in Dr. Jampolsky's estimation, is a *freed* mind. It is not mired in the conflicts of the past. It can assess people and events objectively and remain open to hope, joy, and the possibilities of the future.

Although "forgiveness" is often thought of as a saintly act, it is actually a selfish one. It is something we do for *ourselves,* because forgiving frees us to go on with our lives. The person who does not forgive condemns herself to remain locked in the painful past.

But how does one forgive? I have heard psychologists say forgiveness can take place in an instant, and I believe this is true in many cases. Yet, just as often, forgiveness has seemed to me to be a long-term process. Sometimes I have struggled to forgive someone — have believed that I *have* forgiven them — only to have long-dormant hurts and angers flare up unexpectedly.

Does this mean that I haven't forgiven at all? Perhaps. But instinct tells me otherwise. Instinct suggests I am still in the *process* of forgiving, that part of me has not quite let go of past hurts.

I once heard someone say there are four stages to forgiveness: hurting, hating, healing, and coming together. Anyone familiar with the process of mourning will recognize these as almost identical to the stages of grief. Perhaps that is because forgiving is, in a way, like grieving. When we forgive, we must let go of self-pity, we must give up the desire for revenge, and we must say good-bye to that old, familiar companion — suffering.

• *Hurting* is the first stage of forgiveness. In coping with our own feelings of pain, it's important to remember that *hurt* is a response to *loss.* The deeper the hurt goes, the more significant the loss was to us.

134

Often, an event can summon up hurt out of all proportion to reality. When this happens, we may well be reacting to hurts inflicted on us in the past. For example, the man who is devastated by a minor fight with his wife may not be reacting to her at all. He may be reliving the loss he felt when his mother punished and rejected him for disagreeing with her.

Whenever your hurt seems bigger than the event that triggered it, try using the following process.

1. Ask yourself what you're feeling *now*.
2. Explore the feelings — of pain, helplessness, or fear — that are going on under the surface.
3. Let these "old" feelings carry you back in time. What situation do they remind you of?
4. Explore the old situation. Who were the players? What happened? What important thing (such as love, acceptance, self-esteem, etc.) was taken from you?

Using this process to discover what was lost to you will help you understand your hurt and overcome it.

• *Hating* is a strong word to use to describe the second stage of forgiveness. *Hating* implies that someone is — or ought to be — blamed, and that is not the case. *Anger* might be a better word, for anger is the natural outgrowth of hurt.

Anger comes in two types: constructive and destructive. Destructive anger is twisted by the desire to blame and punish. This is the kind of anger that destroys relationships, causes tension and tension-related health problems, and leaves the individual feeling helpless and impotent. It never goes away but grows larger and more unmanageable as time goes by.

Constructive anger, on the other hand, is not focused on revenge. Rather, it leads the person to ask questions like "Why am I hurting?" and "What should I do to stop it?" This kind of anger gives a person power — power to stand up for herself, power to face the person who has hurt her, power to change the hurtful situation. Once these steps have been taken, feelings of anger dissolve.

When you're angry over hurts inflicted on you in the past, beware of letting that anger become an end unto itself. Far too many people do this. "Letting it all hang out" can be an abuse of anger. Instead of working through the anger, you can be stuck in it and can close yourself off from any possibility of love.

One way to deal with hate and rage is to ask yourself three basic questions.

1. Why do I hate?
2. What do I want to change?
3. What do I need to make that change and let go of the hate?

The wonderful thing about this system is that it is entirely self-contained. Its success depends on you, not on the person who hurt you. Some people resist it for that very reason. They want to make the person who hurt them responsible for their anger. This, however, isn't a realistic goal. The person who did the hurting may never realize what she has done, or she may realize it but be too fearful to acknowledge it.

She may have moved out of your life or — as is often the case with parents — she may have died and left you with no one to confront.

If you ask yourself the three questions outlined earlier, you will quickly see that your anger has a goal: *changing the hurtful situation.* Once you have decided what is needed to make the change, you can go about meeting those needs.

• *Healing,* the third stage of forgiveness, begins when you deal with hurt and anger in constructive ways. Insight and understanding keynote this phase, because — perhaps for the first time — you become aware of certain things about yourself and your life. In the past, pain and anger have kept you in the dark. Now things are sharply in focus.

That's not to say everything will be wonderful. Psychological healing can be painful and uncomfortable, just as physical healing often is. Seeing ourselves, our hurts, and our losses in perspective can fill us with sadness. To expect anything else wouldn't be realistic.

The important thing to remember is that now, at last, we are *seeing* and *understanding.* We are able to look at the hurting spots in our lives without covering them up with indifference, self-pity, or misdirected anger. When we can accept the hurt and loss of the past without letting it interfere with the present or destroy the promise of the future, we have indeed come a long way.

• *Coming together* is the last stage of forgiveness. It means making a complete recovery and carrying on with your life unscathed. Human nature being what it is, many of us refuse to take this step because we feel it will somehow let those who hurt us off the hook. "I want them to see how badly they've injured me," is the way the reasoning goes. This makes about as much sense as refusing to go to the hospital when you've been run over by a car. The only person being hurt is you, and your refusal to get well suggests that you need to go back and work on the earlier stages of forgiveness.

In order to fully recover, you must restore whatever it is that has been taken from you. A person whose abusive parents damaged her ability to love, for example, is not fully recovered until she is able to love again. This is a gift she gives herself, not because it will make her parents feel good but because it will make *her* feel good.

In your own life, make a list of the abilities or choices you feel have been taken from you. Once you have this "loss list" in hand, decide how you're going to fill the gaps. Look for opportunities to exercise your abilities and get back your power. Remember: It's not your fault that you were hurt, but it's your responsibility to get yourself well.

Forgiveness fosters humility, which invites gratitude. And gratitude blesses us; it makes manifest greater happiness. The more grateful we feel for all aspects of our lives, the greater will be our rewards.

Each Day a New Beginning
December 10

We must not join the forces that would put us down or destroy us. Those negative forces are within us more often than they are outside. Wherever they come from, knowing clearly what we want and care about is our strongest defense.

13

Accepting Yourself

Ask any psychiatrist, counselor, or spiritual leader what one of the biggest human problems is and you'll get a unanimous answer: lack of self-esteem. This is tragic because all of us desperately want to accept ourselves and move through life with confidence. We want this so badly we go to great lengths to get it.

We believe that we get self-esteem by

- *disowning parts of the self we feel are unacceptable;*
- *trying too hard to win the world's approval;*
- *creating masks of superiority;*
- *not acting spontaneously but instead acting in ways we hope will be acceptable to others;*
- *avoiding to set some goals for fear we will not achieve them;*
- *denying emotions because they conflict with an idealized view of ourselves.*

The list could go on and on, with only one result: *None* of these ploys works. All of them go *against* the self. In some ways, they deny or disown an important part of our being. As Nathaniel Branden points out in his book, *The Disowned Self,* "Self-esteem cannot be built on a foundation of self-alienation."[1]

Many people resist accepting themselves because they fear it means "giving up." A friend once asked me, "If I accept myself as I am, isn't that like raising the white flag? Isn't it like saying *'This is the best I can do'?"* No, it isn't.

The confusion begins when we are young, when mother or father tells us we are "bad" (unacceptable) for spilling our milk, hiding grandpa's slippers, or pulling the dog's tail. What our parents mean, of course, is that our *behavior* is bad. Few parents have the time or the insight to make this clear to the child. Even if they do, the young mind may not distinguish the difference. Since we want our parents' love, it is likely that any show of disapproval will be interpreted as rejection.

Hence, we incorporate into our life script a strict idea of what "acceptable" is, of exactly what is required to win approval. As we grow up, influences outside the home further embellish and restrict that ideal. Schools, teachers, advertising, the media, and popular culture all contribute to the long list of "shoulds" we carry around inside us. At the moment, the contemporary American woman should be youthful, glamorous, slender, sexy, witty, and well-read; she should be career-oriented without slighting her role as mother, homemaker, and helpmate. Her male counterpart must be tough at work, sensitive at home, available to his children, supportive to his wife, and a dynamo in the bedroom. With unrealistic standards like these, it's no wonder that most of us walk around feeling anything but adequate.

Self-acceptance begins with banishing artificially imposed *shoulds* from your thinking. You don't have to become a doctor to be okay, just because being a doctor is one of the goals your parents set for you. You don't have to *have it all* if having it all is going to put you six feet under. Nor does self-acceptance mean that you have decided to remain exactly as you are today.

Self-acceptance means accepting yourself as a work-in-progress. It means believing that you are okay in spite of your flaws and believing that you have the strength and the power to change.

But where, you ask, is that belief to come from? How can a nonbeliever suddenly become a believer?

One way is to root out the negative messages embedded in the Parent part of your personality. Most of us can close our eyes and let all sorts of voices from the past surface.

"Why can't you be more like your brother?" (Don't be you — be a copy of someone else.)

"You don't have the sense God gave a goose." (You're dumb.)

"Don't touch yourself there." (You're dirty.)

"Can't you ever do anything right?" (You'll never change.)

These voices have become part of the negative Parent within us. We go on listening to them year in and year out, allowing them to bury our self-esteem. But we don't have to. We can replace them with affirmations — fresh and positive messages.

"You are lovable."

"You are kind and caring."

"You have what it takes to succeed."

All of these are examples of affirmations. When you make up your own affirmations, tailor them to counteract the negative messages in your life script.

With a little faith in our own worth, we can choose the calm waters' honesty and apply our creativity to new growth-oriented activities instead of covering up old mistakes.

Today's Gift
December 30

The opinion we have of ourselves isn't just based on beliefs — it's also based on actions. We observe ourselves just as we observe others, and when the belief that we aren't good enough is coupled with actions of self-neglect and abuse, self-esteem sinks even further. The alcoholic who drinks to cover up feelings of inadequacy, for example, will feel even *more* inadequate as he sees himself losing control of his life.

There are certain things each of us must pursue in order to feel good about ourselves. These building blocks of self-esteem are:

- *A sense of worthiness.* Individuals need to see themselves as *deserving* of attention and esteem. The person who sees himself as undeserving will, whether that assessment is true or not, act in self-neglectful and abusive ways.

- *A sense of effectiveness.* No one can feel good about herself if she feels impotent. The person who undermines her ability to act, who becomes a passive onlooker in life, will suffer a loss of self-esteem.
- *Self-regulation.* One of the hallmarks of maturity is the ability to override our impulses. The person who feels that some area of his life is out of control will not respect himself as he respects those who are in control.
- *Meaningful work.* Freud said there are just two things that count in life: work and love.[2] While this is a bit narrow for most of us, work is certainly one of the necessary ingredients for a full life. Work does not always have to be creative, well-paid, or stimulating to be meaningful. A factory worker may dislike her job but find it meaningful because it allows her to care for her family and to maintain independence.
- *Pleasure for pleasure's sake.* Do you remember how good playing made you feel when you were a child? As adults we often lose the ability to play, but we never lose the need or the desire. *Pleasure for pleasure's sake* means playing in the true sense of the word, for the pure joy of it. It means playing golf for the pleasure of seeing the sun on the grass and the satisfaction of hearing the ball roll into the cup — not for the competitiveness of the game or the dividend of talking business at every opportunity.

- *To give strokes.* The exchange of friendly words is the exchange of affection. The person who can give strokes freely and spontaneously will appreciate himself as a caring person.
- *To receive strokes.* How others think of us will affect the way we feel about ourselves. The person who can remain open, who can receive and appreciate the strokes given to her by others, will have a higher degree of self-esteem than the person who feels isolated from others.

When thinking about self-acceptance, it's important to remember that *feelings follow actions*. What you do will influence the way you feel. If you take care of yourself and treat yourself *as if* you are worthy, you will begin to *feel* worthy. And this is true for the other components of self-esteem. If you are having a difficult time directing your thoughts, concentrate on directing your actions — your feelings will follow.

COURAGE
is
the ability
to
strengthen ourselves
against the
fear and despair
of life,
rather than be
drowned by it.

Night Light,
February 17

14

Assuming Risk

All of life's great achievements begin the same way: by taking a risk. The child who tries to walk risks falling on his bottom. The politician who runs for office risks the humiliation of losing by a landslide. The artist who creates something risks being scoffed at. And the person who discloses himself risks being misunderstood and rejected.

While it may be easy for us to risk in other areas of life, it is often extremely difficult to do so in the emotional realm. As Muriel James and Dorothy Jongeward write in their book, *Born To Win,* "In an intimate relationship people are vulnerable, and many times it seems easier to pass time or to play games than to risk feelings either of affection or rejection."[1]

How can we risk-proof ourselves in preparation for intimacy? We can't. Disclosing means risking, and because we risk we will sometimes fail.

Failure has become a heinous word in our culture. We are a nation of winners, and winning is defined in extremely rigid terms. If you watch the U.S. Open on television, the announcer will usually describe just two people: the winner and the loser — even though the "loser" beat hundreds of other contestants to arrive at the final match.

This narrow point of view overlooks one very important fact of life: No one can become a winner without losing many, many times. Lee Iacocca became a popular symbol of success *only* after suffering catastrophic failures. Walt Disney created Mickey Mouse in tribute to the very real mouse who skittered across his floors and shared his suppers during days of grinding poverty. And batting champions like Babe Ruth still hold the dubious distinction of striking out more often than other players.

In her highly insightful book, *Pathfinders,* Gail Sheehy set out to discover what separated pathfinders (people with a high sense of well-being) from people who succumbed to despair and defeat. After interviewing many people and sifting through her findings, she came up with eight qualities essential for pathfinders. Of these qualities she wrote, "The first, the most essential, is a *willingness to risk.*"[2]

Sheehy's pathfinders were not just willing to risk money, time, and involvement — they were also willing to risk *themselves.* They were willing to extricate themselves from safety traps in order to make inner changes — even though those changes incurred discomfort and loss.

In order to become willing to take risks of your own, it's important to understand what you're trying to protect yourself from. Having a concrete idea of your fears will keep them in proportion; letting them lurk in the dark will allow them to grow to overwhelming proportions.

People fear to disclose themselves for many reasons. Here are some of the most common ones. Do any of them sound familiar? If not, take the time to cut your own fears down to size by putting them into words.

- I am afraid of losing control.
- I am afraid of appearing weak and pitiable.
- I am afraid of seeing things about myself that I do not want to see.
- I am afraid of being abandoned.
- I am afraid of being misunderstood.
- I am afraid of being challenged by another.
- I am afraid of discovering a problem I will not be able to solve.
- I am afraid of becoming dependent on someone.
- I am afraid of someone becoming dependent upon me.
- I am afraid of losing respect for myself.
- I am afraid of becoming trapped.
- I am afraid of discovering a need that will be difficult to fill.

There are many ways to deal with fear and anxiety. The simplest and most effective one I have discovered is the three-step plan recommended by Dale Carnegie in his book, *How To Stop Worrying and Start Living.*[3] Although I have paraphrased Carnegie somewhat, the essence of his plan is listed here.

1. *When you decide to take a risk, ask yourself, "What is the worst that can happen as a result?"*

Fears are most powerful when they remain vague. Make up a *worst case* scenario that might come about as the result of your risking. Having a clear idea of the worst that might (and only *might*) happen will prepare you to assume

151

risk. It will put the power in your hands by making the matter one of choice. Say to yourself, "Yes, this might happen, but I *choose* to take the risk."

2. *Prepare yourself to accept the worst — if necessary, losing.*

Are you strong enough emotionally to survive it? Of course you are! Therefore, decide that you are ready to absorb whatever shocks come your way. What you fear may never happen, but if it does, know that it will not do lasting damage.

3. *Decide how you will go forward.*

Make a plan that picks up where your "worst case" scenario leaves off. Know that you will learn something from the situation no matter what happens, and decide to put that newly acquired knowledge to work. Make up your mind that you will not be defeated by individual setbacks. The only way to become a true loser in the game is to let a discouraging experience undermine your willingness to risk again.

Now that you have devised a plan, put it into your subconsciousness. Don't walk around expecting your worst case scenarios to come true. Constantly engaging in catastrophic expectations like these will undermine your resolve and limit your spontaneity. Instead of projecting about the future and what it may hold, live from sunrise to sunrise. Deal with each situation and opportunity as it arises and learn to live, fully and completely, in the here and now.

When we are willing
to be honest, to be humble,
to be learners, to be led
in a constructive direction,
to allow time to be guided
rather than seek instant cure,
then we will learn trust
and will surely make
progress.

15
Learning to Disclose

The secretive person is hampered by old, ingrained behavior patterns. She has learned how to isolate herself from others and how to withhold herself, but she has never learned how to share herself with others.

It's important to understand that self-disclosure is a social skill, not a mysterious rite. Like all social skills, it can be learned, practiced, and improved on. Listed here are six conditions necessary for making successful disclosure.

1. *Honesty.* Self-disclosure means revealing something real and genuine about yourself to another. It doesn't mean distracting yourself or the other person with hypothetical problems and theatrics. Some people have become remarkable actors, churning out high-intensity disclosures that spell significance with a capital *S.* Often, these disclosures are shamelessly self-congratulatory. The would-be writer who never writes, for example, often *confesses* to a fear of success. This is mere stage dressing for the genuine problem — a deep-seated fear of failure.

Dishonest disclosures do a great deal of harm. They keep the discloser from coming to grips with real issues by throwing up a smoke screen of phony concerns. They also deepen isolation and alienation. The person on the receiving end senses that he is being used and the relationship quickly stagnates.

2. *Someone to disclose to.* Someone doesn't mean just anyone. In order to make successful disclosures, you must pick an appropriate other to disclose to. A person can be inappropriate for any number of reasons. Someone you work for or someone who works for you is often too involved in your business life to be a good candidate. Also a poor candidate is the person whose time, understanding, or willingness to listen are severely limited. The worst choice of all is the person who listens for ulterior motives — to play armchair psychologist or engage in a game of confessional one-upmanship.

Intimacy does not just depend on your ability to disclose — it also depends upon the person who receives that disclosure. Eric Berne called this *bilateral intimacy* and described it as a "candid, game-free relationship, with mutual free giving and receiving and without exploitation."[1]

3. *A sense of time and place.* Many people engage in disclosures without regard to anything else that's happening around them. The woman who unburdens herself to a new acquaintance is likely to frighten that person away, closing the door on future intimacy. The husband who attempts to discuss an important issue with a wife who's harried and exhausted is likely to meet with disappointment.

Just as there are appropriate and inappropriate people to disclose to, there are appropriate and inappropriate opportunities in which to make disclosures. The person who pays no attention to this is either woefully self-absorbed or subconsciously trying to thwart the intimacy she thinks she's seeking.

4. *A spontaneous approach.* The open person does not approach an encounter bent on self-revelation. She has no set speech in mind and no well-rehearsed life history on her lips. Disclosing oneself doesn't mean aggressively explaining who you are and what you're all about. Rather, openness is the absence of defensiveness. It is the ability to be yourself in the presence of another. It's important to remember that not all disclosures are made with words. Spontaneous actions and reactions often speak volumes, where studied words would only interfere.

5. *Reasonable expectations.* What do you expect to get in return for sharing yourself with another? Healthful and productive disclosures are made without high price tags. Of course, you hope that the person you disclose to will be receptive and empathetic, but expectations that go beyond that are likely to meet with disappointment.

The person who repeatedly feels cheated or let down after making disclosures may be filled with unrealistic expectations. She may expect the other person to become responsible for her problems, to take them on as if they were her own. Or she may hope that the other person will make a personal commitment of love or support. Expectations like this fall into the realm of game-playing: *I'll disclose myself in order to get this or that in return.* This thinking is self-sabotaging. It loses sight of the fact that self-disclosure is a worthy goal in and of itself.

Our emotional well-being is enhanced each time we share ourselves -- our stories or our attentive ears.

Each Day a New Beginning
April 10

6. *Receptivity.* Intimacy does not happen all at once. It develops slowly, through the ritual of sharing. As intimacy grows, people make increasingly significant disclosures to one another. At first the stakes are small — you tell someone about the day you had, he tells you what his day was like. But as time goes on and disclosures are swapped back and forth, the stakes escalate. Soon you are sharing thoughts and feelings that are much more personal and self-revealing.

It's important that you learn to play both roles — the giver and the receiver. If you only know how to make disclosures but don't know how to receive them, you will thwart the ritual of sharing necessary for true intimacy.

Being open to
contact with
our world,
    keeping our
    barriers down
    so we stay
    in touch,
restores our
awareness
of purpose.

16
Moving Ahead

Reading, reflecting, and gaining insight into one's problems are wonderful pastimes. But they don't amount to much unless you're able to put them to productive use. Deciding to become more open is one thing, but putting that decision to the test of action requires great courage.

Turning your life script around is difficult — as difficult as rechanneling the course of a river. In order to make lasting changes, you will need to arm yourself with four things: motivation, information, a plan of action, and patience.

• *Motivation* is the ingredient that makes all things possible. It enables people to overcome great obstacles and triumph against the odds. Too often, people lose sight of *why* they want to make changes. They go around feeling punished and rebellious, and soon they return to their old, comfortable behavior patterns.

Instead of giving yourself dead-end messages such as, "I must become more open," use statements such as, "I *choose* to be more open because. . . ." Remind yourself of the benefits that come with self-disclosure. This will boost your motivation and give you a positive goal to work toward.

• *Information* is what this book has been designed to give you. Don't expect to have absorbed everything at once. If you feel foggy about certain points, go back and read those sections again. Try paraphrasing what you have read, using examples and insights from your own life to reinforce the concepts.

Although I have tried to give you useful information, it cannot match the information you have about yourself. Most people are quite capable of healing themselves. They know the answers to their questions, even though they're often unaware of it.

As you have read this book, some answers about your own life have probably become clear to you. Pay attention to these newly discovered insights. If possible, spend some time writing about them — not just because they might slip away from you if you don't — but because writing itself will deepen your understanding.

• *A plan of action* is your blueprint for change. Saying that you are going to be more open is not enough. You must also decide what you are going to do to achieve that end. For example, if you have gone through life covering up something about yourself, you might decide to share that secret with another person. Or you might choose an easier first step. If you are prone to isolating yourself from others, you might choose something as simple as going to visit someone or asking someone out for coffee.

The plan you devise is up to you, and there are only two criteria needed to make the plan a successful one: First, that each step challenges you and, second, that each step moves you closer to your goal.

Remember, too, that plans can be experimented with. If you find yourself stuck in a certain point or find that something isn't working right, go back to the drawing board and start again.

• *Patience* is the ingredient most people forget. They're so anxious to get going that they expect everything to happen at once. Although psychologists occasionally speak about the "one-session" cure, this is extremely rare. Usually, even the most highly motivated individual has a difficult time changing.

It's important to remember that the behavior patterns of a lifetime do not vanish at the wink of an eye. Those patterns have come to pass because they serve a purpose. Over a period of time, they have become deeply ingrained habits.

If you expect change to come too quickly or too easily, you risk losing faith in the process and in yourself. You may become discouraged with yourself, question your ability to change, and give up on yourself completely.

As you are changing, you need to have patience with yourself. It will not always seem like you're making progress, and sometimes you won't be. At times you'll lose your footing and fall backwards.

I've already discussed the phenomena of baby steps earlier in this book. The baby takes a step, totters and falls, only to pull himself up and begin again. Eventually, he learns to walk, not because each step was a success but because he is always ready to *try again*.

You can reach your goals in exactly the same way — by taking as many baby steps as you need to and always allowing yourself to try again.

REFERENCES

Chapter 1

[1]Eric Berne, *What Do You Say After You Say Hello?* (New York, New York, Bantam Books, 1972).

Chapter 2

[1]Daniel Goleman, *Vital Lies, Simple Truths: The Psychology of Self-Deception* (New York, New York, Simon and Schuster, 1985), pp. 29-54.
[2]Fritz Perls, Ralph Hefferline, and Paul Goodman, *Gestalt Therapy* (New York, New York, Dell Publishing Co.,Inc., 1951).

Chapter 5

[1]William Wordsworth, "Ode: Intimations of Mortality from Recollections of Early Childhood," *Wordsworth* (New York, New York, Penguin Books, 1971), pp. 71-77.
[2]Eric Berne, *What Do You Say After You Say Hello?* (New York, New York, Bantam Books, 1972).

Chapter 7

[1]Dr. Srully Blotnik, *Otherwise Engaged: The Private Lives of Successful Women* (New York, New York, Penguin Books, 1986).

Chapter 8

[1]Eric Berne, *What Do You Say After You Say Hello?* (New York, New York, Bantam Books, 1972).

Chapter 10

[1]Stansfield Sargent and Kenneth Stafford, *Basic Teachings of the Great Psychologists* (Garden City, New York, Dolphin Books, 1965), p. 188.

Chapter 11

[1]Eric Berne, *What Do You Say After You Say Hello?* (New York, New York, Bantam Books, 1972).

[2]Rollo May, *The Courage To Create,* (New York, New York, Bantam Books, 1976).

Chapter 12

[1]Gerald Jampolsky, *Love Is Letting Go of Fear,* (New York, New York, Bantam Books, 1981).

Chapter 13

[1]Nathaniel Branden, *The Disowned Self,* (New York, New York, Bantam Books, 1972), p. 72.

[2]Sigmund Freud, *General Psychological Theory* (New York, New York, Macmillan Publishing Co., Inc., 1963).

Chapter 14

[1]Muriel James and Dorothy Jongeward, *Born To Win,* (Reading, Massachusetts, Addison-Wesley Publishing Co., 1971), p. 62.

[2]Gail Sheehy, *Pathfinders,* (New York, New York, Bantam Books, 1982), p. 95.

[3]Dale Carnegie, *How To Stop Worrying and Start Living,* (New York, New York, Pocket Books, 1953).

Chapter 15

[1]Eric Berne, *What Do You Say After You Say Hello?* (New York, New York, Bantam Books, 1972), p. 25.

READING LIST

Casey, Karen, with illustrations by David Spohn, *The Love Book,* Center City, MN, Hazelden Educational Materials, 1985.*

Casey, Karen, and Martha Vanceburg, *The Promise of a New Day,* Center City, MN, Hazelden Educational Materials, 1983.*

Cordes, Liane, *The Reflecting Pond,* Center City, MN, Hazelden Educational Materials, 1981.*

Dean, Amy E., *Night Light,* Center City, MN, Hazelden Educational Materials, 1986.*

Each Day a New Beginning, Center City, MN, Hazelden Educational Materials, 1982.*

Malerba-Foran, Joan, *When I Was Your Age,* Center City, MN, Hazelden Educational Materials, 1984.*

Missildine, W. Hugh, *Your Inner Child of the Past,* (New York, New York, Pocket Books, 1982).

Rubin, Theodore Isaac, *Compassion and Self-Hate,* (New York, New York, Ballantine Books, 1983).

Today's Gift, Center City, MN, Hazelden Educational Materials, 1985.*

Touchstones, Center City, MN, Hazelden Educational Materials, 1986.*

Twerski, Abraham, M.D., *Self-Discovery in Recovery,* Center City, MN, Hazelden Educational Materials, 1984.*

---

*Available from Hazelden Educational Materials, Box 176, Center City, MN 55012-0176. (1-800-328-9000)

Of Course You're Angry

by Gayle Rosellini and Mark Worden

Those of us in chemically dependent families often have special problems with anger. It's no wonder. Feeling anger is a normal, healthy emotion. Yet learning to express anger appropriately is difficult for families experiencing the escalated fear, guilt, and unpredictability in chemically dependent homes. *Of Course You're Angry* offers specific guidelines for learning healthy ways to acknowledge and express our anger.
(72 pp.)
Order No. 1169

Healthy Relationships Series

by Brenda Schaeffer

These four pamphlets written by licensed psychologist and transactional analyst Brenda Schaeffer explore the benefits and pitfalls of love relationships. This series provides solid, supportive help for all of us seeking healthy, mature love. Each pamphlet includes case histories, specific detailed exercises, and checklists to help us know if what we're feeling is love or addiction.

Love Addiction:
Help Yourself Out	Order No. 5208
Power Plays	Order No. 5205
Signs of Addictive Love	Order No. 5207
Signs of Healthy Love	Order No. 5206
All four pamphlets	Order No. 5903

108-9